HIGH O

HIGH

on

HAWTHORN

The road to the

2013 PREMIERSHIP

PHILLIP TAYLOR

NERO

Published by Nero,
an imprint of Schwartz Publishing Pty Ltd
37–39 Langridge Street
Collingwood Vic 3066 Australia
email: enquiries@blackincbooks.com
http://www.blackincbooks.com

Copyright © Phillip Taylor 2014
Phillip Taylor asserts his moral right to be known as the author of this work.

All Rights Reserved.
No part of this publication may be reproduced, stored in a retrieval system,
or transmitted in any form by any means electronic, mechanical, photocopying,
recording or otherwise without the prior consent of the publishers.

National Library of Australia Cataloguing-in-Publication entry:

    Taylor, Phillip Ross, author.

    High on Hawthorn : the road to the 2013 premiership / Phillip Taylor.

    9781863956628 (paperback)

    9781922231482 (ebook)

    Taylor, Philip Ross.

    Hawthorn Football Club.

    Football fans--Victoria--Anecdotes.

    Australian football--Victoria--Anecdotes.

    796.336

For my sons, Oscar and Declan,
and in loving memory of my father, Peter.

CONTENTS

INTRODUCTION

As Jane Austen wrote before the 2013 AFL premiership season, "It is a truth universally acknowledged among football pundits that Hawthorn will win this year's AFL premiership."

This proposition was based on data such as the average age of Hawthorn's playing list compared to other recent premiership-winning teams; the relative mix of youth and experience; the return from injury of key players; the presence of star players Buddy Franklin and Cyril Rioli; strategic, targeted recruiting; and the devastating hurt felt from 2012's narrow Grand Final loss to Sydney.

All reasonable tea-leaf signs, of course, but many Hawk fans were certain of 2013 premiership glory on altogether sturdier empirical grounds: it was our turn! We'd finished third in 2011 and second in 2012, so in any sort of pattern-recognition algorithm you care to program, surely we would finish first in 2013.

I began this book to track our progress through the 2013 season and review each game as I experienced it, whether that be from the ground, watching on TV, listening on the radio, getting score updates online or just crank calls from opposition fans. After coming within reach of glory in 2012, I wanted to record our path back to premiership redemption in 2013.

You could argue there is already an oversupply of uncalled-for commentary and unsolicited speculation about football. And you'd be right. There are more television hours of analysis and review than there is actual game-time each week. But while there are more than enough outlets from which to get stats about kicks, corkies, handballs and hard-ball gets, this book aims to give expression to a dramatic and eventful season from the fans' perspective, to give voice to the exhilaration and exasperation, the anxiety and excitement that your average Hawks enthusiast experienced over a period that engendered both the blackest and brightest of emotions.

Football has always been important to me. I collected and swapped footy cards like other kids when I was young. I played in the yard at school and acted out my own matches at home. But it wasn't just the game and the players that attracted me; I loved the colour, the flags and floggers of the cheer squads, the streamers and cut-up paper they threw when their team scored a goal and of course the banners the team ran through before each match. I studied the messages on them as if they were scripture.

It wasn't just football in general that interested me, more specifically I loved Hawthorn. My mum barracked for Melbourne and, as a result, my three brothers and I were all nominally designated Demons fans. But I remember one night in what would have been 1969 or 1970, when I was five or six years old, my parents took all of us to Melbourne Sports Depot (MSD) at Chadstone Shopping Centre to buy new football jumpers. We were permitted to buy any team we wanted, and while my brothers chose Richmond's black jumper with yellow sash, perhaps tempted by the fact that they were one of the top teams at the time, I recall being instantly enamoured of the jumper with the brown and gold vertical stripes.

So I left with a Hawthorn jumper, though at the time I'm not sure I was aware which team it was. For me, the decision was as much sartorial as anything else, which might say something about my sense of fashion.

As it happened, given that we lived in Melbourne's south-eastern suburbs, Hawthorn was more or less the local team. Of course, what I didn't realise at the time, but which my brothers found fairly regular occasion to remind me, was that Hawthorn wasn't a very good team and generally languished somewhere near the bottom of the ladder.

All that changed in 1971, however, when, largely through the agency of superstar full-forward Peter Hudson, Hawthorn started winning regularly. So much so that they reached the Grand Final to play St Kilda. Better still, my uncle, an MCC member, took me to the game. I still recall thinking how smart Hawthorn looked when they ran out – how the overcast sky somehow made the gold of the jumper more vivid.

I also recall being in tears at three-quarter time with the Hawks trailing by 20 points and begging my uncle to take me home. I couldn't bear to watch any more. But as any Grand Final historian will testify, Hawthorn staged a dramatic final-quarter comeback to win by seven points. If I wasn't already rusted onto the Hawks before the match, I was by the end.

Then in 1973 a family friend bought me a Hawthorn membership and began taking me to the matches. I sat with the cheer squad in the Grandstand at Glenferrie Oval and joined in the chanting and cheering. I've been going regularly ever since and have witnessed the great Hawthorn eras of the '70s and '80s, celebrating the string of premierships and Grand Final appearances. I helped make the banners for many years and spent most of my September school holidays cutting up brown and gold crepe paper, and most Saturdays waving it.

Now I have two sons, Oscar and Declan, who both follow Hawthorn, with the eldest, Oscar, joining me at the games. Even my nephew and niece, Max and Zoe, are on board as Hawthorn members, so the love of the brown and gold now crosses family lines and generations.

For 40 years Hawthorn's on-field fortunes have dictated my mood and outlook from week to week. After we narrowly lost the

Grand Final to Sydney in 2012, I was plagued all summer, reliving moments from the match in my mind, revisiting our missed shots on goal and squandered opportunities. I was tormented by visions of Sydney scoring, their players and fans celebrating.

I tried to present a calm, relaxed façade. I pretended to be philosophical about the loss, to view it with a sense of sang-froid: it's only a game, the better team won on the day, we didn't take our chances – that sort of thing. As if I was a normal, functioning adult with perspective, composure and a life to be getting on with. But I didn't believe it. The reality is I was a mess, groping about in the dark for direction and purpose, which I knew I wouldn't attain until Hawthorn could redress 2012's Grand Final miscarriage.

As the 2013 season wore on, so did the Essendon drugs scandal and Buddy's contract speculation. And with Hawthorn and Geelong jostling at the top of the table, there was the growing realisation that to win the premiership Hawthorn was going to have to overcome its nemesis and the most famous football hoodoo of the modern era.

In any year that the Hawks have hoisted the cup I've had tears in my eyes. But in 2013, they streamed down my face in a heady cocktail of joy, redemption, relief and the realisation that at last I could get on with my life.

This is the story of how it happened.

PARADISE LOST, PARADISE REGAINED

Hawthorn 2012 to 2013

The new AFL season of 2013 is upon us and, like most football pundits, my thoughts have turned to the poetry of John Milton. In the seventeenth century he prophesied Hawthorn's tragic loss in the 2012 Grand Final in his epic poem "Paradise Lost" – 12 books of verse that tell the story of the fall of man, from the temptation of Adam and Eve by Satan to their expulsion from the Garden of Eden and descent into hell.

A clearer allegory of the 2012 Grand Final you couldn't hope to read. The 12 books represent the year 2012, and though his surname is not given, it is quite clear that "Adam" is Adam Goodes. Milton even predicts the lasting effect that this match – or, as he paints it, our descent into hell – has on Hawthorn fans, asking, "What hath night to do with sleep?"

But he assuages us as well with a vision of a better dawn: "This horror will grow mild, this darkness light."

He even offers some inspirational titbits that Hawthorn coach Alastair Clarkson, or "Clarko", could include in his pre-match address ahead of the Round 1 game against Geelong: "Awake, arise or be for ever fall'n."

And should we meet Sydney again in the big one, Clarko might like to burst forth with:

What though the field be lost?
All is not Lost; the unconquerable will,
And study of revenge, immortal hate,
And the courage never to submit or yield.

As long as the boys pick up on the key phrases "revenge" and "immortal hate" they should be fine.

So while "Paradise Lost" gives an unhappy account of the 2012 Grand Final, it does contain clues of future redemption, none more so that the sequel, "Paradise Regained", published in 1671 – an even 300 years before our second flag. Coincidence? You decide.

"Paradise Regained" is based on the Gospel of Luke (Hodge, captain of Hawthorn) and his account of the Temptation of Christ – a fairly straightforward parable about Satan (rival clubs) trying to tempt Christ (Buddy Franklin) with better offers. Whereas in "Paradise Regained" Satan tempts the starving son of God with a banquet, riches, earthly glory and wisdom, AFL media outlets circulated reports of Greater Western Sydney, Carlton, Collingwood, Sydney, Fremantle, West Coast and possibly other clubs courting Buddy with similar blandishments, although earthly glory is surely not something he's ever lacked. But "Paradise Regained" also plays on the idea of reversals: thus, all that is "lost" in the original poem (the 2012 premiership) is "regained" in the follow-up (the 2013 premiership).

A deep textual analysis of "Paradise Regained" will reward attentive readers with many similar parallels between the fate of man and the fate of Hawthorn. Reading the two poems together not only reminds us of what occurred in 2012, but also, more tellingly, reveals what will occur in 2013 – a Hawthorn premiership as told in the Gospel of Luke Hodge.

"MALCESKI DOES MURDER SLEEP"

Milton's existential enquiry "What hath night to do with sleep?" is not the only literary antecedent that speaks to Hawks fans in the wake – and I use the word in all of its meanings – of the 2012 Grand Final, for no lesser figure than Shakespeare also offered a hint of our future when he wrote:

> *Sleep no more!*
> *Malceski does murder sleep, the innocent sleep,*
> *Sleep that knits up the ravell'd sleeve of care,*
> *The death of each day's life, sore labour's bath,*
> *Balm of hurt minds, great nature's second course,*
> *Chief nourisher in life's feast ...*

For what Hawks fan hasn't been jolted awake by a sudden and bloodcurdling vision of Sydney Swan Nick Malceski's 2012 match-sealing goal floating through the big sticks? And once awake, who can regain innocent slumber without first rolling through a loop of truly shocking moments from the same match: Buddy's two first-quarter misses, Sam Mitchell giving away 50 metres and a goal when all the momentum was with the Hawks, Buddy and Jack Gunston's final-quarter misses, Clinton Young tripping over his own feet in the goal square to allow another Sydney goal ... on it goes in an endless horrifying loop.

"The mind is its own place, and in itself can make a heaven of hell, a hell of heaven," wrote Milton in "Paradise Lost". Or, equally, it can just make an ongoing hell. In the days and weeks after the 2012 Grand Final my mind, to the exclusion of all other thought, simply replayed these horror moments from the match.

English writer Martin Amis estimates that the average heterosexual male experiences approximately 1000 "sex thoughts" a day, from idle, passing notions when a pretty girl walks by, to deliberate, full-blown fantasies about desirable women. In the weeks after the Grand Final, I was operating at a similar ratio, but instead of thinking about lingerie and lipstick, I was dwelling on Grand Final passages that turned bad. Indeed, it took all of the 2012–13 summer for these dark imaginings to dwindle to a manageable handful of GF horror moments. And thank God, because now I can finally get back to my allotted quota of sex thoughts and fantasies ... just in time for Round 1.

THE YOUNG AND THE RESTLESS: CLINTON YOUNG DEFECTS TO COLLINGWOOD

Footballers make strange decisions during games. You've only got a nanosecond to locate a target and execute your kick or dish off a handball before being tackled by some sweaty oaf, so it's no surprise that players panic and fumble or make the wrong decision.

But outside the pressure of a match situation, when you've got time to consider all of the factors, weigh up the whys and why nots, and deliberate over the moral rights and wrongs of any given range of possibilities, it becomes surprising, if not unthinkable, that between the 2012 season and the 2013 season, a nice, polite Hawthorn player with a neat haircut, no visible tatts and all of his teeth would choose to move to Collingwood. Of all teams!

I mean, I get it if a player wants to return home, or is offered the captaincy somewhere, but to just move to Collingwood? To fall back on the age-old complaint, who can understand the Young?

As a rule, I don't boo former Hawthorn players who move to other clubs. To have worn the brown 'n' gold into battle is perhaps the highest achievement to which any human can aspire – well, short of enjoying a torrid night of passion with Scarlett Johansson or P.J. Harvey, that is. Or both.

I'm always happy to see former Hawks succeed, whether they've been delisted, returned home or just want to seek out greater opportunity at another club. But to leave Hawthorn to go to Collingwood is charting a whole new and shadowy moral path. As my friend Chan-Tha said, "He's dead to us now."

Even worse, I read an article where Clinton Young talked about using the 2012 Grand Final loss to Sydney as a spur for greater success this year. Hold on! That's our Grand Final loss – not Collingwood's. He can't appropriate our tragedy for Collingwood's dark purposes. How dare he! Instead, perhaps Clinton Young should reflect on the fact that if he hadn't fallen over in Sydney's goal square while chasing the ball during the final minutes of the match, allowing the Swans to score a crucial goal, then we might have been in a position to salvage the game and actually win the Grand Final!

I won't spit on him as he walks down the race (after all, I'm not a Collingwood fan), nor do I wish serious injury on him (though I do think in making his decision he might have at least considered Hawthorn's patience and expense when he was out injured for the best part of two seasons). And while I may not boo him when he collects a possession against us, I might emit a lo-fi hum of disapproval.

LAKE'S ENTRANCE: BRIAN LAKE JOINS HAWTHORN

Our big signing over summer has been Bulldog defender Brian Lake. The basis for this signing was that we need a big defender to deal with "monster forwards" such as Adelaide's Kurt Tippett and Collingwood's Travis Cloke, who both played well against us in the 2012 finals and whom Ryan Schoenmakers ("The Cobbler"), was unable to deal with by himself. Of course, we won our respective finals against Adelaide and Collingwood, and then lost to a team without such a "monster". But now that Tippett has gone to Sydney, we may yet need Lake in a big game this season.

Lake has already distinguished himself by getting arrested in Sorrento over summer. It's not unheard of for a high-profile player to have a couple of drinks too many on a balmy summer evening; it's not even that unusual for such a player to become involved in a scuffle or a fracas of some sort; nor is it particularly uncommon or remarkable that such a player might get himself arrested over such an incident; but where Lake distinguishes himself is that not only he was arrested but also his wife! That is particularly impressive!

I must admit to being sceptical when we first recruited Lake – it seemed to be a media-driven decision, as if football journalists like Craig Hutchison were in charge of recruitment – but it could be that both Brian and his better half are bringing to the club the sort of ruthless "no-holds-barred" attitude that we need to succeed. In any case, I'll happily eat my words if my scepticism proves to be unfounded.

SAVE THE FRANKLIN: LANCE FRANKLIN PUTS OFF CONTRACT NEGOTIATIONS

The biggest story over summer at Hawthorn becomes Buddy Franklin's decision to hold off the renegotiation of his contract until the end of the season. A straightforward enough business decision, you'd think, and an announcement that pretty much draws a line under the topic. If only ...

As the football media keep repeating, this decision simply represents the new reality of free agency. If that is the case and this will become commonplace, then why don't the media accept their own analysis and stop banging on about it?

Quite aside from whether this issue is becoming a distraction for Hawthorn and Franklin, it's certainly becoming a bore for the rest of us.

On a single day, apropos of nothing, Jake Niall has an article in *The Age* about how there are not yet any offers from rival clubs. Of course not ... because he's under contract to Hawthorn for a whole season yet. There's no story. Niall has written 12 paragraphs saying that there are no developments in this story. So another way to approach this reality might be to write nothing. Just putting it out there, Jake Niall, Caroline Wilson et al.

This follows revelations that Franklin was drunk and "out of sorts" at the Grand Prix. Journalists were quick to link this incident to his decision to put off contract talks, tracing a pattern of wayward behaviour that will see him leave the Hawks. Instead, it should be viewed in its correct context – which is, what else is there to do at the Grand Prix but get drunk? Once you've seen a couple of cars speed past, not a lot changes. Getting drunk at the Grand Prix is not only understandable, it's really the only normal response to being there. Buddy was just behaving as any rational person would: "God, this is dull; pour me another schnapps."

Referring to movie stars of the 1950s with whom he was intimate, American author James Salter writes in his memoir, *Burning the Days*:

> The truth is, in stars, their temperament and impossible behaviour are part of the appeal. Their outrages please us. The gods themselves had passions and frailties – these are the stuff of the myths; modern deities should be no different.

I don't know how to interpret Buddy's decision to put off contract talks, but it might simply be that he thinks he'll be worth more at the end of another season. It might be that if he can win another premiership with Hawthorn he'd consider going back to WA, or it might be that he wants to take a year off to trek around South America, run with the bulls in Spain, work with the poor in Calcutta or solve the Middle East crisis. All of them will be just fine with me, so long, of course, as he kicks 100-plus goals and we win the flag.

And as long as he doesn't go to Collingwood, Carlton, Essendon or Sydney.

THE 23 ENIGMA

How the number 23 foretells Hawthorn's 2013 premiership triumph

It's a truism to say that the number 23 carries great significance at Hawthorn. There are the three Cs: Crawshay (Simon), Collica (Michael) and Crawford (Justin), but of course we all recognise it as the number worn by some of our most celebrated champions: John Peck, Don Scott, Dermott Brereton and, for 2013 at least, Buddy Franklin. All of them great players, as we know, but more than that, all four of them epitomise individual flair and play or played with an aura of unpredictable brilliance that carried match-winning potential. It's fair to say that in each of Hawthorn's great eras and in each of our premierships, we've had a great number 23.

Of course, then you consider the great number 5s (5 being 2+3): Peter Crimmins, Andy Collins and Sam Mitchell. Add in Leigh Matthews (who originally wore number 32, which of course is 23 in reverse) and you start to appreciate the full power of the number 23 and realise that it is more than just two digits slapped on the back of a jumper.

It is not only at Hawthorn where the number 23 is seen as having special life-changing properties. There is, in fact, a school of belief – more a cult, really – that all significant events and incidents are related in some way to the number 23. For some it is a good omen,

ξnifies disaster. This phenomenon is known as
is chapter we'll look at some of the factors that
gma and demonstrate just how this foretells
premiers in 2013.

........erican author William S. Burroughs is widely thought to be the original proponent of the 23 Enigma. He relates the story of a Captain Clark who operated a ferry between Tangiers and Spain. Captain Clark told Burroughs that he'd been running the route for 23 years without an accident. On that very day the ferry sank, and later that evening Burroughs heard a radio report about the crash of Flight 23 on the New York–Miami route. The pilot was another Captain Clark.

From that moment, Burroughs started collecting occurrences of 23s, an activity since taken up by many others, most relentlessly by science-fiction writer and futurist Robert Anton Wilson in his series of books written with Robert Shea, *The Illuminatus! Trilogy*.

More recently, actor Jim Carrey has championed the 23 Enigma, starring in a film called *The Number 23* about this phenomenon and naming his production company JC23 Entertainment.

So that makes a comic actor, a cosmic conspiracy theorist and octogenarian junkie – there's a trustworthy trinity if ever there was one. And Burroughs, I need hardly point out, died at the age of 83 – a Hawthorn premiership year.

The people in the subculture who follow these beliefs, of which Hawks fans must count themselves, refer to themselves as twenty-thirdians. Their belief in the magical properties of the number 23 stem from a series of cosmic crossovers and occurrences that suggests a pattern and even a model for human existence – that's if you need any further evidence than the Pecky, Scotty, Dermie and Buddy quartet.

Seventeenth-century scholar Archbishop Ussher published a chronology of existence showing that the Earth was created on Sunday 23 October 4004 BC. He's quite specific about the Sunday, though he doesn't say if the job was done in time to catch *Modern Family* that night.

The Mayans, meanwhile, believed that the world would end on 21 December 2012 (and as you may have worked out, 2012 is 20 + 1 + 2 = 23). This didn't, of course, come to pass, which is good, because otherwise we wouldn't be in a position to win this year's flag.

But there are other signs linking the number 23 to the end of the world. Rasputin predicted the world would be engulfed by fire on 23 August 2013 – the 23 is quite clear in this prediction, and you'll recall that 2013 is 20 x 1 + 3 = 23. If you want to be picky you might argue that, well, the world didn't actually end on 23 August 2013, but you know Rasputin was writing 100 years ago so perhaps from that far out we can take it as meaning give or take a year. I don't think we can question the 23, though.

Also, a new comet known as ISON is growing alarmingly brighter in the sky, assuming you have a powerful enough telescope to see it, that is. It was discovered by Russian astronomers in September 2012 – not only does 9 + 2 + 0 + 12 (where September is the ninth month) = 23, but, as we know, September 2012 is a particularly ominous date for Hawthorn. As the comet gets closer to our solar system and sun, it is tipped to grow very bright indeed. The link between the comet and the end-of-the-world prophecy harks back to a prediction of Nostradamus that "the Pope to replace Benedict XVI will 'flee Rome' in the month of December when the sky has two suns". Well, we've got the Pope (Francis), the Catholic Church is in a state of near collapse, and the second sun is on its way, so perhaps we should check the Pope's forward bookings.

As you can see, the number 23 is inextricably linked to the very existence of the planet, central to both the creation and the destruction of Earth. And not just the beginning and end, but between these two cataclysmic events, while it's still spinning (and though this ostensibly takes 24 hours, I'm sure there's a calculation involving leap years, the date line, daylight savings and depreciation to show that it's really 23), the Earth is doing so while tilting on an axis of 23.5 degrees.

Not only that, but the Tropic of Cancer is located at 23.5 degrees north while the Tropic of Capricorn is at 23.5 degrees south. And if you think these .5s throw out the theory, remember that 5 is 2 + 3: 23.

Not only is the number 23 intrinsic to our host planet, but also to the life that thrives on its surface. Each parent contributes 23 chromosomes to the fertilised egg, while it is the 23rd chromosome that determines gender. Furthermore, the physical human bio-rhythm cycle is 23 days, plus it takes 23 seconds for blood to circulate through the human body. Now, I haven't measured these, obviously, and certainly my own blood feels more sluggish, but, on this, like global warming and why left-footers are better kicks, I'm just going to have to trust the experts. Which means that, not to put too fine a point on it, without 23 there is no humanity (which may sound a tad hyperbolic, but it isn't news to Hawks fans).

In numerology the number 1 represents the individual or the leader; number 2 represents balance and duality (right/wrong, black/white, and, dare we say, brown/gold), while number 3 is the product of 1 and 2, the innovative creative force, the best of individualism and balance – sounds like Buddy on the run lining up a long-range goal, really.

There are, of course, other signs: Michael Jordan and Shane Warne, the two best practitioners of basketball and cricket respec-tively, both wore 23. David Beckham, arguably one of the greatest soccer players ever, wore 23 for Real Madrid and LA Galaxy and then wore 32 (23 in reverse) for AC Milan. Current Hawthorn coach Alastair Clarkson himself wore 23 when he played for Melbourne. So number 23 is clearly associated globally with sporting prowess.

Kurt Cobain was born in 1967 (1 + 9 + 6 + 7 = 23) and died in 1994 (1 + 9 + 9 + 4 = 23), and with Nirvana released his landmark album *Nevermind* on 24 September 1991 – Grand Final week in a Hawthorn premiership year.

All of this is fascinating, but how does the 23 Enigma necessarily relate to the AFL, and, more importantly, to Hawthorn? Well, to extrapolate some of the more obvious connections: there are 18 teams in the AFL from 5 different states: 18 + 5 = 23. In season 2013, which of course is 20 x 1 + 3 = 23, there are 23 rounds of football and each team is named with 22 players + 1 coach: 22 + 1 = 23.

So, having established that the number 23 is intrinsic to the AFL, let's now look at how this reveals Hawthorn as the 2013 premiers. It is five years since our most recent premiership, in 2008, five being 2 + 3. Plus, there have been 23 premierships decided since our famous victory in 1989.

In fact, Hawthorn has won 10 premierships: 1961, 1971, 1976, 1978, 1983, 1986, 1988, 1989, 1991 and 2008. If you add the single integers together, i.e., 1 + 9 + 6 + 1 + 1 + 9 + 7 + 1 etc, you get 229, and then divide by the number of premierships we've won, 10, you get 22.9, which, when you round it up, equals 23.

It's also worth noting that the distance from Hawthorn's home in Wellington Road, Mulgrave, to the MCG on Punt Road, Richmond, where the Grand Final is played, is, you guessed it, 23 kilometres.

And do I need to add that the 23rd Prime Minister of Australia was Bob Hawke, who not only has a name that is evocative of Hawthorn, but was elected to government in the Hawks premiership year of 1983 and left office in another Hawks premiership year of 1991, thus encompassing our most successful era, and, in fact, the most successful era of any club in the history of football?

And talking of the history of football, there have been 116 premiers between 1897 and 2012. However, there have only been 114

Grand Finals – with no final being played in either 1897 or 1924 (both, incidentally, years in which Essendon was crowned, so we're not going to them. I don't know why they do – the bloke who did their salary cap in the 1990s must have been on premiership count as well). So the Grand Final has been won 114 times: 1 + 1 + 4 = 6; add in the 6 times Hawthorn has been runner-up and you're up to 12, then add the number of premierships we've currently won, 10, and you get 22, plus add the one we're going to win in 2013, and there you go, 23! And I don't think that's drawing too long a bow – do you?

As all Hawks fans are acutely aware, we should have won the premiership in 2011 and 2012, suffering agonisingly close finals losses in both years; add 11 and 12 together and, you guessed it, you get 23.

Of course, the real 23 Enigma is Buddy Franklin himself. Will he stay with Hawthorn or will he leave? Or does it all depend on the numbers in any new contract offers?

THE HALLOWED TURF AT HIGHGATE –
HAUTE COUTURE IN CRAIGIEBURN

PRACTICE MATCH – HAWTHORN V NORTH MELBOURNE
Highgate Reserve, Saturday 16 March 2013

Footy season was upon us in a matter of minutes. Just a few days after a record-breaking hot spell for March of eight days above 32 degrees, we were still enjoying balmy autumn weather when the ball was bounced for Hawthorn's pre-season practice match against North Melbourne at Highgate Reserve in Craigieburn.

I live a covert life in the enemy territory of Essendon, and as this was to be Hawthorn's only appearance on our side of town, my son Oscar and I decided to trek out along the Hume Highway to Craigieburn to see the boys get into shape for the 2013 season.

Such was the unseasonal heat that we were clad in just shorts and T-shirts and we delayed our departure while we applied the necessary sunscreen. By the time we arrived at Highgate Reserve, however, the temperature had plummeted, the wind was up and driving rain was spearing us as we walked into the ground. Footy season had arrived while we were in the car!

The Hawks were four goals to two in front when we arrived, and there was a decent crowd: a couple of thousand Hawks fans and a couple of hundred North fans. The field looked good and there was a pleasant old-style suburban footy atmosphere, with kids kicking footballs on the grass embankment and a mass pack forming behind the goals every time a player lined up a shot, which naturally enough turned into a sprawling stacks-on pile as kids fought over the ball – until security arrived, of course. All it lacked were cars parked around the boundary sounding their horns to applaud goals.

You could tell the weather had turned by the fact that the queue for coffee was longer than the queue for beer. But an even longer queue formed in the third quarter of Hawthorn players taking their turn to line up for goal.

The Hawks fielded a reasonably full-strength side, although there were a few players that looked unfamiliar – number 32, number 37 and number 35, and a few whose names I'd forgotten, but of course the big number 23 was there.

Watching Buddy take the field in Craigieburn is like seeing Radiohead play the Ferntree Gully Hotel. There's something incongruous about seeing a thoroughbred like Buddy in a place like Craigieburn – he's certainly the most glamorous thing to ever hit the area. At least since the Hume Freeway was built.

As for the North Melbourne side, who other than North fans would know whether they put out a full-strength team? Drew Petrie and Brent Harvey were there, but I didn't recognise the others; they could have been rookies or 200-game veterans for all I know. It's no surprise that Harvey and North were behind the push over summer to have the players' names printed on the backs of jumpers, as no one knows who the North players are. Most likely Harvey doesn't know their names either and was pushing this agenda so he knows whose name to call for the ball.

A decent half-time lead to the Hawks blew out in the third quarter as they capitalised on the strengthening gale-force breeze that brought the ball inexorably forward. Buddy marked strongly and slotted a couple, although you couldn't help but wonder where he would have been without the sage advice of the pundit on the fence who, between sips of VB, gave Buddy directions ("Bud, drop back, drop back. Bud, go right, mate, go right."). As if someone who's won two Coleman Medals and kicked over 100 goals in a season can't read the play and requires personal coaching from a bloke on the fence sucking cans.

And our man was emblematic of the fashion sense prevailing in Craigieburn. On the eve of the L'Oréal Melbourne Fashion Festival, it was apparent that the look for men was trackie-daks and ill-fitting T-shirts, while for women, black leggings worn as pants was de rigueur. Admittedly, the unexpected cold snap had forced me back to the car, where the only garment I could rustle up was a white towel that I draped about myself cape-style. So I don't criticise Craigieburn couture with any sense of superiority, but it is perhaps telling that I still seemed to be the only one making an effort.

As the third quarter came to an end, a looming black cloud grew ominously blacker – apocalyptically black, in fact – and given the Hawks were 70-odd points in front and we were freezing, we decided to head off back down the Hume. And lucky we did, because minutes later the cloud opened up in a biblical downpour that rendered driving nearly impossible, let alone playing football. The wind was so strong that Hawthorn was actually kicking straight.

I subsequently heard the match was abandoned halfway through the final quarter, ostensibly because of the risk of injury, but quite possibly the Hawthorn players were simply growing uneasy about leaving their luxury cars unsupervised for so long. I mean, how long can a Lexus or an Audi, to say nothing of a Ferrari, remain undisturbed in the badlands of Craigieburn?

Final scores: Hawthorn 19.8.122 d North Melbourne 5.11.41

GROUNDHOG DAY

When I was a teenager, the Valhalla Cinema in Richmond showed the cult movie *The Blues Brothers* every Friday night at 11.30. If you happened to be in Church Street around that time, you'd see the moviegoers milling out the front of the cinema wearing their Blues Brothers uniform of black suit, white shirt, skinny tie and felt trilby. This wasn't a momentary fad for a month or two: it lasted for years. It was only because the cinema shut down that it stopped at all.

And it wasn't that the audience for this movie was so vast or varied that it required repeated screenings to deal with surging demand, or that the cinematic concepts were so complex and multi-dimensional that repeat viewings were required to uncover new layers of subtext and meaning. It was the same people turning up every week to watch the plot unfold in exactly the same way, to witness the same characters say and do exactly the same things at the same junctures, to sing the same songs and feel the same emotions they felt at every previous viewing.

Likewise, in the 1993 movie *Groundhog Day* Bill Murray plays a TV weather presenter who finds himself reliving the same day over and over again. And so it is with Hawthorn and Geelong fans, who turn up to the MCG twice a year (in their considerable tens of thousands, it should be noted) to relive the same match, to witness the same teams follow more or less the same script with only slight variation each time. It's tight, fortunes ebb and flow, Hawthorn holds a slight edge at some stage, only to miss a few opportunities and be overrun by a persistent Geelong outfit, with Jimmy Bartel making a significant contribution, and the Hawks ultimately losing by one to 10 points.

When the final siren rang in this 2013 Round 1 match with the Hawks seven points behind, I felt exactly like Bill Murray's character felt every morning when the digital clock flipped over from 5.59 to 6.00 to mark the dawn of yet another Groundhog Day.

When basketball began to grow in popularity, I was not alone in noting that you may as well start each game with both teams level on 80 points and five minutes remaining, because pretty much every game comes down to that anyway. You could do the same sort of thing with Hawthorn and Geelong: start Hawthorn on 85 and Geelong on 70 and say, "Right, there's five minutes left." You'd still end up with the same result – Geelong by one to 10 points. If they know their job, you have to assume the marketing department at Geelong is considering putting together a box set of these final quarters.

The objective viewer (which, I hasten to point out, is not a thinly veiled autobiographical guise I'm adopting) might point out that it was a great game, with both teams going in hard and showing a mix of aggression and sublime skill. This objective viewer might highlight Joel Selwood's courage and inspirational play, Sam Mitchell's midfield supremacy and ball getting, Paul Chapman's class, Brad Sewell and Paul "the Poo" Puopolo's endeavour, Mitch Duncan and Jimmy Smedts's poise under pressure, Bradley Hill's dash and Buddy's athleticism, and conclude that it was yet another Hawks–Cats classic.

Of course, they'd be right, this objective viewer, but I ask, is there anyone more irritating than an objective observer of the game highlighting that your calls for "Ball!" are misguided, that Buddy's free kicks are a bit fortunate, that "Gee, that Bartel's good, isn't he?"

and worse, "Yep, the Hawkers blew that one ... they really should have won it"? I almost prefer the crazy old Cat fan who, as he headed for the exit, turned to no one in particular, and the Members' Pavilion in general, to bellow in angry tones more suited to a domestic dispute, "Go you Catters!"

APRIL FOOLS

On the eve of the 2009 AFL season, then Hawthorn president Jeff Kennett commented that Geelong didn't have the mental toughness to beat Hawthorn. Smug and still slightly surprised after our victory over them in the '08 Grand Final, most Hawks fans agreed. Of course, in the nine subsequent encounters since that pronouncement, we haven't won once. Worse, in most of them, we could have or should have won. This inability to beat Geelong has become known as "the Hawthorn hoodoo" or "Kennett's curse".

For more than four years since the infamous Kennett curse, the Hawks have been Geelong's bunnies. And now that Hawthorn and Geelong are routinely scheduled to play on Easter Monday, we've simply become their Easter bunnies.

There we were, five goals in front halfway through the second quarter, with our midfield and defence on top, our forwards breaking even, and even the umpires giving us all the chocolates, but in keeping with the predictable plot lines of these Groundhog Day matches, we all knew what was going to ensue. And it duly did. Geelong was always going to win, and again we were just their bunnies in an elaborate April Fools' joke. Ha ha.

Hawthorn is never more vulnerable than when a few goals in front of Geelong at half time. The only bet worth taking at such a stage is how long it will be before Geelong hits the front or which Geelong player will step up to kick the winning goal.

In the end, the seven-point margin flattered Hawthorn. We were completely outplayed in the second half and our little flurry near the end never really threatened to amount to much. I'm almost relieved that Luke Breust missed a set shot a minute or so from time so that it didn't turn into yet another sub-goal loss. That is something I really don't think I'd have coped with.

I'm just glad Geelong doesn't have the mental toughness to defeat Hawthorn, as Jeff said – imagine how much they'd win by if they did.

HERNIAS AND HAMSTRINGS

I had an operation scheduled for the day after the match to correct an abdominal hernia. During a pre-operative consultation with the surgeon I issued strict instructions that if the Hawks have lost another close one to the Cats, he should just rip out my heart while he's in there. However, it feels like the Cats have beaten him to it.

As surgery goes, this is supposedly routine, but as with any surgery involving a general anaesthetic there is an element of risk. Even so, in the lead-up to the weekend I was dreading the match much more than the surgery. The surgery would at least make me better.

Hawthorn fans, I feel, are divided into two types: those who watch the '08 Grand Final ahead of matches against Geelong as a sort of mood setter or preventative pill, and those who watch it as a purgative or panacea after we've suffered another narrow loss to them. I tend to the latter, so had the DVD handy in case I needed it during my post-operative recovery.

There's very little point giving any sort of match description; we've seen it all before. But purely from a record-keeping perspective, it may be worth noting that our first goal of the season came from Jordan Lewis. Brad Sewell picked up where he left off in the 2012

Grand Final as our best player, Bradley Hill was lively in the first half, Schoenmakers played quite well to win his share of contests and Buddy kicked a couple of great second-quarter goals.

In the second quarter, when Cyril Rioli received a free kick for a high tackle – a Geelong player was sitting on Cyril's back with his arms over his shoulders, so the umpire's decision seemed fairly self-evident to me – it was amusing to see Joel Selwood, of all people, complain to the umpire for awarding a free kick for a high tackle.

But he didn't complain nearly as much as the Cats fan in the row in front of me, who became apoplectic at various points through-out the match – most vociferously whenever Buddy strayed into the action, wishing all manner of afflictions to befall him. At one point he shouted out in a demented scream that he hoped Buddy would "do 20 hamstrings". My knowledge of anatomy is not comprehensive so I'm not sure how many hamstrings a person has, but at a guess I would say one or two in each leg. I'll have to ask my surgeon. Clearly, this bloke imagines Buddy to have some sort of concert-harp-type set-up in the back of his leg. Unless he's simply hoping for the same hammy to recur 20 times.

It soon became a moot point, because by the final quarter he'd upgraded his seething curse to "I hope you die, Buddy". It seemed a pretty severe threat to lay on someone who'd tried hard and kicked a couple, but then certain people must have said the same thing to Jesus at about this time of year as well. This type of abuse must come with being seen as a saviour, I suppose.

I did wonder if this is the type of anti-social behaviour at matches we're exhorted to report, but instead I decided to rise above such ugly sentiments and not get involved, for fear the surgeon would have more than a hernia to fix the next day.

Watching the Hawks didn't exactly help my prognosis. They tried hard but were just outplayed by a good team. It might also take me a few matches to reacclimatise to the new all-gold-back jumper that has replaced the white patch with black number. I was impressed, however, by young Jed Anderson, whose second involvement in his first game was to run straight into an oncoming Cat to make a contest. He didn't win it but he certainly didn't shy away from the contact.

THE PROMISED LAND

After the 2008 Grand Final, Geelong forward Paul Chapman is reputed to have vowed that they'd never let Hawthorn beat them again, and certainly he's been as good as his word, but I'm not sure it's up to him any longer. I feel it's moved beyond that and is now actually a pathological condition ... it's the Hawks that won't let themselves beat Geelong.

In Christian mythology, Easter starts with the unpleasant bit – Christ being crucified and the shops being shut – and finishes on a good note – Christ's resurrection and the Easter Bunny dispensing chocolate eggs. My Easter was the reverse: it started with a stirring and uplifting Springsteen concert at Hanging Rock and concluded with a dispiriting and depressing Hawthorn loss to Geelong. Even though we've grown accustomed to losing to the Cats in recent years, and I've had to squirm through each iteration of the curse, I look forward to the day when we eventually beat them again, as we will, as we must, and reach the promised land of which Springsteen sings.

Final scores: Geelong 13.15.93 d Hawthorn 12.14.86
Ladder position: 11th
What we learned: In the 2013 season opener between Carlton and
    Richmond, it took only 20 seconds for the umpires to pay
    Chris Judd his first free kick of the year.

Richmond is sitting on a goldmine if it could actually win the flag. After just one win there was more Richmond branded merchandise being worn at Hanging Rock than there were Bruce Springsteen T-shirts. You could have been mistaken for thinking the Tigers were about to take the stage.

What we already knew: It would take less than 30 seconds of the 2013 season for the umpires to pay Chris Judd a free kick.

HAWKS ON HEAT

The news during the week was dominated by the mad bellicose ranting and absurd posturing of hostile political forces and mad despots. First there was Kim Jong-un moving his ballistic missiles into range of South Korea and Guam, and then, more alarmingly, there was Jeff Kennett firing his own ballistic missiles by advocating that Hawthorn sack coach Alistair Clarkson after our seven-point opening-round loss to Geelong.

Um, Jeff, it was Round 1 and it was only seven points.

To sack our coach after one loss of just over a goal would elevate us to the bizarre levels of elite soccer, where coaches are changed like bandages. In 2012 Chelsea sacked its coach after winning the UEFA trophy as the best team in Europe – it's unclear what more the coach could have done, really ... got Chelsea a seat in parliament? Won the Eurovision Song Contest?

Sacking Clarkson after one narrow loss, however, would certainly send a strong message to any would-be applicants for the vacant position. If this is Jeff's standard, you just wonder what he would advocate for Melbourne and Mark Neeld. Two losses totalling 200-plus points would surely warrant sacking, plus perhaps onselling him to the white slave trade, or harvesting and trafficking his organs. Or has Melbourne devised an even more cunning and dastardly plan by making him continue to coach their hopeless rabble of a team?

This was the set-up to our now must-win encounter with the Eagles: the Hawks coming off a six-day break, compared to a 15-day break for the Eagles, and temperatures topping 32 degrees in Perth. At least our all-white clash strip was going to prove nice and cool in the heat.

"KEDDIE TO FULL FORWARD!"

Not that I could see it. I was stranded on the couch as a post-op invalid, and with no Foxtel I was stuck with the radio for this match. Radio station SEN was covering the match and my DAB+ was picking up a nice clear signal. A lively and chatty commentary team was at the helm – Gaz, Gossy and Brett (they referred to each other exclusively by nickname so their real identities remained a mystery to me) – but they seemed only marginally biased by WA broadcasting standards.

They were also reasonably accurate, in that I usually had some idea at which end of the ground the action was taking place and which team had the ball – although both sides having a Hill playing for them (Bradley for the Hawks and Josh for the Eagles) caused some confusion.

Plus I learned that Steffi Graf is still good-looking, or "goes alright", as one of them put it, though apropos of what I can't say, and that Asher Keddie had been backed in from $11 to $1 for the Gold Logie, which was being presented that night. A good omen, perhaps, as Keddie is a famous name at Hawthorn from the 1971 Grand Final, and with her bouncy blonde locks Asher would look good in the brown 'n' gold verticals (and the shorts). She would also have fitted nicely into our mid-'90s line-up alongside our blond contingent of Shane Crawford, Justin Crawford, Rayden Tallis, Paul Hudson, Daniel Chick et al.

For expert analysis and expostulations I had my Hawthorn buddy Chan-Tha relaying messages via text. Chan-Tha was watching via Foxtel and was also at home in post-op rehab (our operations were unrelated; it wasn't some sort of Siamese-twin separation or existential Grand Final angst operation – for while that wound is real enough, it is sadly inoperable).

Chan-Tha is a work colleague and we became friends through our mutual love of Hawthorn. On any given day she's the most stylishly dressed person in the room, and this was never more evident than the day we first spoke, when she was wearing the famous brown and gold verticals on a "wear your footy colours to work" day. From expansive conversations at each other's desk on a Monday morning about the previous weekend's match, or which players she saw shimmying at Boutique nightclub, we progressed quickly to sitting together at Hawthorn matches, leaving our respective footy-agnostic spouses to their own devices while we hovered somewhere between the pocket and the wing of the MCC Members', or, depending on how the match was progressing, taking refuge in the Bullring or Blazer bars.

Chan-Tha can shout louder than me and has an equally acute sense of when the umpires are denying Hawthorn natural justice. So she was perfectly placed to balance the WA crowd bias with an acceptable and welcome Hawthorn bias.

Without being able to see the action, the parochial Eagles crowd provided the radio follower with a clear picture of which team was awarded the free kick, much quicker than the commentators could ever have hoped to describe it. The sound of nearly 40,000 people moaning was truly heart-warming. And positively joyous when they became completely feral in the final quarter.

IT'S ... IT'S ... THE HAWTHORN BLITZ

With the effects mic unable to pick up any cheering Hawks fans, every goal came as a complete surprise when it was announced. And there were plenty of them. It was a veritable roll call of Hawthorn goals: Rioli, Breust, Buddy, Roughead, Buddy, Rioli. Then Burgoyne, Smith and Rioli again, and the Hawks were blitzing.

Of course, anyone who follows Hawthorn, or even just saw the previous week's match, knows that we are always vulnerable once we've gained a solid lead. And so it proved, with the Eagles slamming on four goals in quick succession, before Breust and Roughead both goaled to give us a 68–42 half-time lead. As our scoreline of 11.2 suggested, we were kicking uncharacteristically straight. It must have been Perth's heat, or maybe I was in a painkiller induced delirium.

When Rioli and Buddy opened the third quarter with quick goals I could again relax in my sickbed, though my wound was troubling me again as the Eagles began to edge back into the contest. As the third quarter progressed, we started to miss goals and the Eagles were kicking accurately. Breust missed a shot right on the siren. "Fuck" read Chan-Tha's text. Our three-quarter-time lead was only 19 points and, according to the SEN boys and, more tellingly, Chan-Tha's text messages, we were looking tired. I hit the Tramadol hard.

Listening via radio, it can be difficult to tell who's playing well. The commentary team assured us Mitchell was playing brilliantly. His name wasn't being called that often, but most of his best work is so quick and deft that commentators don't have time to mention him, lest they miss the guy scooting off with the ball. Or in one case when they said, "Roughead lumbers after the ball" – a picture instantly familiar to any Hawks fans.

Brad Sewell, Max Bailey and Grant Birchall seemed to be in the action and, reassuringly, Luke Hodge's name was being called with increasing regularity as the game wore on. He appeared to be repelling a number of Eagles attacks and set up a telling goal late in the third with a great tackle and rebound. It was developing into the most welcome comeback since Bowie released "Where Are We Now?", his first single in 10 years and, coincidentally, the exact question Hawthorn might have been asking had Hodge not been there.

PASS THE PANADEINE FORTE

So I had Tramadol and Panadeine Forte to help get me through the final quarter, but as it turned out, e's and wizz would have been better suited as the Hawks piled on the goals: Grant Birchall and David Hale to start with. Then Hale again, followed by Breuuuust to wrap up the game.

Getting into the spirit of things, the umpires awarded Bradley Hill and Buddy free kicks plus 50-metre penalties, both resulting in goals that sent the crowd into frothing convulsions of hate. "Love it," texted Chan-Tha.

Listening to the Subiaco crowd baying, the commentary team felt the need to virtually apologise for them and reassure listeners that with a free-kick count of 23 apiece (there's that number again), the umpiring was not the reason the Eagles were 44 points down. Then Breust and Buddy iced the game with a couple more goals.

There are fewer forms of pain relief as effective as a 50-point win against the odds. With our first win, the season could now be said to have commenced properly and we could realistically begin contemplating the 2013 premiership.

Final scores: Hawthorn 23.10.148 d West Coast 15.8.98
Ladder position: 9th
Number of texts exchanged during the match: 65

What we learned: Steffi Graf is still hot, apparently. Asher Keddie to take home the Gold Logie (which she did). And, after Essendon defeated Melbourne by 148 points at the MCG, those cynics who said Round 1 simply showed that Essendon is still on drugs and Melbourne is still tanking might actually be on to something.

What we already knew: Jarryd Roughead doesn't run, he lumbers.

HAWTHORN ... HEAVEN SENT

ROUND 3 — COLLINGWOOD V HAWTHORN
MCG, Sunday 14 April 2013

Two new heroes emerged for me in 1976 on different sides of the world. In Australia David O'Halloran, a bandy-legged left-footer, made his debut for Hawthorn. He took his place on the half-back line alongside club legends Peter Knights and Ian Bremner and went on to win best first-year player, the forerunner of today's much feted Rising Star award, and play in a premiership in his debut season.

In the UK Johnny Rotten burst into the public consciousness with his band The Sex Pistols and the sound of punk rock, shaking up the music scene and penning such classics as "Anarchy in the UK" and "God Save the Queen", and becoming public enemy number one along the way. He was the ultimate cultural villain.

I loved them both and they were each in the news in the lead-up to the Round 3 fixture between Hawthorn and Collingwood.

David O'Halloran, aka Rubber, sadly passed away during the week of the game. He wore number 8 and played 180 games for Hawthorn, including two premierships (1976 and 1983), and was the prototype for the long-kicking, left-foot half-back flanker that is now synonymous with Hawthorn.

As if in tribute to O'Halloran, Hawthorn selected young Taylor Duryea on a half-back flank to play his first match. Shorter than

O'Halloran, he is nonetheless known for his long, accurate, left-foot kick and he will hopefully go on to enjoy as long and distinguished a career as David O'Halloran.

R.I.P. Rubber – an eternal Hawthorn champion.

Johnny Rotten, aka John Lydon, took to the stage in Melbourne on the Thursday night before the match with his post-Pistols band, Public Image Ltd, or PiL, and played a cracking show of arch, post-punk art rock. But it wasn't this gig that made the news. Earlier in the week Johnny endeared himself to the Australian public with a petulant outburst on Channel 10's show *The Project*, telling host Carrie Bickmore several times to "shut up" and embarking on what many perceived to be a sexist rant.

If *The Project*'s producers and panel had done their research, they should have been aware that Johnny doesn't play the role of demure, polite guest. And you certainly don't interrupt him when he's holding forth and opining in his definitive way. He was simply reverting to type and they allowed him to play to his gallery, consisting mostly of himself.

Johnny offending the hosts of *The Project* was as sure a bet as Buddy stealing the show against Collingwood, which he duly did. Equally predictably, the chorus of disapproval for Johnny's rant would be easily surpassed by the moaning of Collingwood fans complaining of some perceived slight by the umpires.

SOMETHING'S ROTTEN

Talking of public image, the Hawks took to the field in a new away strip – our third outfit in as many matches. This one features a brown patch on the back of the jumper on which sits a gold number. Like some society dame, Hawthorn simply refuses to be seen wearing the same thing twice. On this occasion we teamed it with a black armband as a tribute to David O'Halloran, but at this rate it won't be long before we go retro chic and don the infamous navy number with a brown and gold harlequin pattern from the mid-'90s night series, an outfit so garish even jockeys would refuse to wear it.

There had been a double blow at selection, with Brad Sewell, one of our most industrious midfielders, ruled out, while for Collingwood, Nick Maxwell, historically one of our surest avenues to goal, was also missing.

And early on it looked like these absences would be telling. Collingwood was using the ball cleverly and combining well, while Hawthorn was second to the ball, slipping, sliding and spilling marks. A great team goal for the Pies involved six slick handballs and culminated in Jamie Elliott kicking his second goal for the quarter.

Collingwood was dominating early play and created multiple scoring opportunities, whereas Hawthorn managed only two first-quarter goals: one from a free kick to Bradley Hill and one to Shaun Burgoyne after a move that had originated in a free kick to Jordan Lewis. This came courtesy of a typical act of petulance from Collingwood's Heath Shaw, who grabbed the scruff of Lewis's jumper and pulled him to ground. Judging by the white noise of the hooting, it's fair to say that the Collingwood fans didn't necessarily agree with these decisions.

The pattern continued in the second quarter and became alarming when Collingwood led by 22 points, with Travis Cloke and Jamie Elliott having kicked three goals each. Meanwhile, their Hawthorn counterparts, Buddy and Luke Breust, had none between them.

I was at the match with my son Oscar, Chan-Tha and friend Julian, a Collingwood supporter who regularly joins me for this fixture. Julian was thoroughly enjoying the action and was in full voice celebrating Collingwood's early supremacy. He is, however, a realist, and had been to all three Hawthorn v Collingwood matches in 2012, in which Hawthorn had prevailed easily, so knew that such a lead was not yet definitive. Insistent rain drove us from our seats in the open to an undercover perch high on level four. These seats afford a similar view of the playing arena as Felix Baumgartner had when he took his edge-of-space skydive from the Red Bull Stratos capsule in 2012. So, while you miss the thwack of flesh on flesh in the tackling, you do have a great vantage point to study set-ups, systems and strategies. The problem was that Hawthorn didn't seem to have any. Instead, all I could see were gaping holes through which Collingwood could swing the ball forward to where Cloke was one-out against Schoenmakers.

Either Breust was playing a blinder – setting up the lo-fi Hawthorn hum of "Breuuuuuust" – or the Collingwood fans were finding fairly regular fault with the umpiring and booing at every stoppage. It was unclear if there was a specific decision that upset them, or whether they were afflicted by some sort of Tourette's instinct to boo.

Listening to the Collingwood crowd moan, I thought back to Johnny Rotten's directive to Carrie Bickmore on *The Project* and just wanted to tell them to "shut up".

Julian was the first to sniff a change in the wind, and with no discernible shift in ascendancy, somehow Hawthorn got back into the match with three quick goals: first new boy Jed Anderson snapped truly, then Buddy marked strongly from a speculative Burgoyne punt, and finally Hodge took it from a stoppage and got onto a 50-metre spiral punt that went sailing through.

It was half time and despite being outplayed for much of the game, we were only one point down.

HAWKS RISE

Alastair Clarkson can't have been happy at half time, and in line with the chorus of PiL's biggest hit, "Rise" – check it out on your preferred streaming service – he found a way to transmute this anger into energy, as the Hawks were a different team after the break.

The three Bs – Breust, Buddy and Birchall – banged on goals early in the third term, and with energy and enterprise the Hawks were beginning to get on top. Hodge was becoming the most influential player on the ground; Josh Gibson, Ben Stratton and Grant Birchall were controlling the back line; debutant Taylor Duryea was becoming more assured with the ball; and Sam Mitchell was in every pack.

Although Julian had given the match up as lost by this stage, when Cloke slotted a behind with 8:25 to go in the third quarter, Hawthorn led by just one goal, 10.9 to 9.9, and it looked to the rest of us like we were in for a tight finish. Until the next passage of play ...

Brent Guerra took the kick-in, launching a torpedo into the centre square. Stratton marked it and played on immediately, but was tackled by Sam Dwyer. As they fell to the ground Stratton handballed to a running Franklin, who hurdled their prone bodies and slammed the ball on his boot from about 75 metres out. The ball landed in the vacant goal square and bounced through. It had taken just 12 seconds from post to post, and I was thankful for our position high up on level four, from where we had the best possible view of the goal.

After a goal like that there wasn't much chance that we'd lose. Collingwood cheer squad identity Joffa could have safely donned his cabaret-style, gold lamé jacket and held aloft his "Game Over" banner, as he does when Collingwood is in an impregnable position. If those who judge the goal of the year weren't so obsessed with the now bog-standard dinky rolling banana goal, they might like to consider this one in their adjudications. Or the next one ...

Hodge grabbed the ball from a stoppage and sent through another 50-metre torp, post-high. This was followed in quick succession by goals to Roughead, Burgoyne and, right on the siren, Breust. Three-quarter time and the Hawks led 15.9 to 11.9 and were looking strong.

The final quarter commenced with a goal off the ground from Buddy and the Hawks continued to edge ahead, adding six more goals to make it 15 goals to six in the second half, or 18 goals to six if you count back from that moment with five minutes remaining in the second quarter when Hawthorn trailed by 20 points. Throughout the onslaught the giant screen at the ground repeatedly focused on Collingwood president Eddie McGuire and Joffa looking glum as they watched on. I feel sorry for Eddie and Joffa never being able to watch a game in anything like privacy, and I'm certainly glad the TV cameras don't seek out my reactions whenever Hawthorn is losing – I tend to look like a cross between Edvard Munch's *The Scream* and Picasso's *Weeping Woman*.

So comprehensive was this 55-point triumph that the Collingwood fans – those who had stayed – could barely muster a boo by the end.

There are not many things more enjoyable than watching the Hawks steamroll Collingwood. Watching Australian television personalities squirming in uncomfortable befuddlement at Johnny Rotten-type rudeness comes close, but really, he was just being belligerent for the sake of it, so it was hard to take his side. The PiL gig on Thursday night, however, was every bit as powerful as Hawthorn's second-half performance, and I sang along as lustily to his post-punk anthems as I did to the Hawthorn theme song at the end of the match.

Final scores: Hawthorn 22.13.145 d Collingwood 13.12.90
Ladder position: 6th
What we learned: Johnny Rotten hasn't mellowed. Jed Anderson
  may well be our next Mitchell, and despite a couple of errors,
  Taylor Duryea played a strong debut game. Plus his name
  rhymes.

What we already knew: That Luke Hodge bloke goes alright, doesn't he? There was news in the week after the match that a woman obsessed with Hugh Jackman threw a shaver full of her pubic hair at him as some sort of tribute. I'm not saying I'm kinky, but if Hodge keeps turning it on like he did this week, I can't promise I won't get out the Lady Bic myself.

THE HODDLE STREET END AT AURORA

The overlap of the Hawthorn v Fremantle match in Launceston with the Richmond v Collingwood match at the MCG set up possible confrontations in pubs showing games on Fox Footy. Not wanting to become embroiled in disputes with publicans and patrons about which match should be shown on their big screen, and fearing I'd be outnumbered and out-feralled, I arranged to watch the game with other like-minded Hawks fans at Chan-Tha's house.

Sure, Channel 7 was showing the match on delay, but who can watch second-quarter action unfolding in a time warp when a frantic final term might be underway? So Oscar and I jumped in the car and set off for Chan-Tha's. And besides, her TV is so big the players are actually larger than life. Even the Poo looks tall.

Of course, this necessitated driving from Essendon to Richmond, through several iterations of roadworks and detours, plus the inevitable football traffic converging on the MCG. So the trip took one and a half hours, roughly twice what it would have taken to fly to Launceston to watch the game in person. As a result, we ended up listening to the first quarter on SEN in the car.

Thanks to the miracle of Optus TV, however, we were able to

relive the first-quarter action later. And it was worth doing so. In the opening seven minutes the Hawks didn't manage a single entry inside 50, but in the ensuing five minutes, thanks largely to Cyril Rioli, we'd got it in there five times and scored 4.1, all of which happened while I was stuck on a small stretch of Hoddle Street.

FREEZING OUT FREO

The great thing about playing Fremantle in Launceston is that it takes the Dockers an entire quarter to thaw out – a fact highlighted by Tom Harley on Channel 7 when he informed viewers that on each of their past three visits to Launceston, Fremantle failed to kick a goal in the first quarter. So Aurora is not so much a fortress for us, but a sort of ice cave that immobilises unwitting teams from balmier climes, just like Mr Freeze's hideouts in Batman.

One of Fremantle's first-quarter behinds came from a free kick to their ruckman, Jonathan Griffin, after a ruck infringement against David Hale. It was hard to spot the infringement, but in explaining the reason to Hale, the umpire seemed to say that it was because Hale was "looking at" the Fremantle ruckman. Now, my knowledge of the finer points of the rules is probably sketchy, but I was previously unaware you could be penalised for looking at your opponent. Really, a decision like that deserved a goal.

LIFE OF POO

The umpires weren't the only ones making strange decisions (and I should point out here that I have no argument with the umpires. If anything, Hawthorn is getting a better deal this season than ever before – just ask the Collingwood supporters). Far stranger was Buddy's decision when running into an open goal – about 10 metres out – to handball over to the Poo in the goal square, where he was duly mown down by Stephen Hill and the ball bobbled across the line for a point.

Moments later, the Poo took a great mark on the line and attempted a banana kick, which flew across the face of goal and snuck in for another behind. So in the space of two minutes, the Poo had two shots at goal from an aggregate distance of about five metres, and scored two points.

Fortunately, Buddy reassessed his priorities and the next time he gathered possession, just outside 50, he bombed it through.

LIFE OF SCHOE

More disturbing was Ryan Schoenmakers going down early in the second quarter with a season-ending knee injury. The "much maligned Schoenmakers", as he has become known by football commentators, was playing well when he buckled his knee after being edged out of a contest by Fremantle's Kepler Bradley. Not since former Hawk Zac Dawson was repeatedly outmuscled one afternoon by Collingwood's Anthony Rocca has a player copped so much criticism for being outmarked by an opponent a foot taller, but Schoenmakers did a pretty good job each week and had been playing well this year.

His injury was a particular shame at this point because he had got his hair to sit with just the right sort of jaunty foppishness that could see him cast in *Brideshead Revisited*.

Schoenmakers' absence was just one reason why Fremantle was getting back into the game. Indeed, after Hawthorn established a 30-point lead by quarter time, the margin barely strayed from that figure, hovering somewhere between 24 and 36 points for much of the game.

With the game in a sort of stasis, the casual viewer had more time to focus on the peripheral action. The regular cutaways to the respective coaching boxes showed Alastair Clarkson and his two male lieutenants in constant animated conversation, while an expressionless woman, sitting impassively alongside them, focused intently on her monitor, seemingly oblivious to whatever conversational flurry was blustering around her. Meanwhile, Fremantle Dockers coach Ross Lyon could be seen with just two empty chairs for company, but seemed to be muttering away incessantly. Was there anyone in the box with him, or had he driven them away with his bemoaning?

BURGOYNE FETISHISTS

Dennis Cometti and Bruce McAvaney take the mike for Channel 7's *Friday Night Footy*, while Brian Taylor and Luke Darcy ("BT and Darce") call prime-time Saturday-night matches. That left us with Channel 7's C team of Basil Zempalis and Hamish McLachlan to call this Saturday-afternoon fixture, with former Geelong captain Tom Harley providing expert commentary. Tom knows what he is talking about and offers astute analysis of the match, but some of the other commentary was insightful for all the wrong reasons.

After Shaun Burgoyne kicked his second goal, Harley and fellow special-comments man Craig Bolton inventoried some of his many qualities as a footballer, such as his work as a midfielder and his accurate finishing, to which Zempilas added, "An immaculate-looking footballer, isn't he, Burgoyne – he wears those socks so high."

Now, do I detect a wee tinge of regret from an ankle fetishist, or is it just that Basil has an eye for well-worn hosiery? Imagine how impressed he'd be if he saw Burgoyne in fishnets. And what do you think he makes of Burgoyne's nickname, "Silk"?

Continuing on the Burgoyne theme (and the reason they were obsessing over Burgoyne, I might add, is that, along with Grant Birchall, he was playing a fantastic game), Hamish McLachlan added, "Very difficult name to say fast repetitively, Shaun Burgoyne. Say it five times really quick."

Firstly, the degree of difficulty seems relatively low to me, compared to saying, for example, Basil Zempilas Basil Zempilas Basil Zempilas Basil Zempilas Basil Zempilas. Or even Hamish McLachlan Hamish McLachlan Hamish McLachlan Hamish McLachlan Hamish McLachlan. And secondly, I'm puzzled at the circumstances whereby someone might be compelled to say 'Shaun Burgoyne' five times in quick succession ... unless you're dashing past him on the wing calling for the ball, of course, and it's my guess that neither Basil or Hamish will ever be in that position.

Both commentators also seemed mightily impressed by the coincidence of two brothers, Stephen and Bradley Hill, playing for opposing teams, despite this phenomenon being relatively common-place in the era of the draft – the Selwoods, the Reids, the Tucks, the Reiwoldts (okay, they're cousins, but you get the point).

Hamish went on to say, "The Hill brothers – sounds like you're describing a winery in the Barossa Valley." Clearly the cold and a fairly mundane match were beginning to get to Hamish by this point and he was yearning to quaff a rich and full-bodied Shiraz on the flight home. But even so, I would have thought that with two Western Australians under discussion, perhaps Margaret River might have been a more appropriate wine region to reference.

SOMEONE SHOW BASIL A MAP OF TASSIE

And I shouldn't overlook Basil's opening gambit at the beginning of the telecast: "Welcome to beautiful Hobart." So beautiful it looks like

Launceston. He tried to make up for it by saying "Launceston" incessantly for a few minutes afterwards, just to prove he knew where he was, but it was too late – he'd already put his size-12 foot in it by then.

He may or may not realise the ferocity of the north–south rivalry in Tasmania, but it's a bit like a touring rock band playing in Melbourne and saying "Hello, Sydney!" Someone really needs to show Basil a map of Tassie.

BEND IT LIKE CROWLEY

The friendly and well-intentioned prattle of Basil and Hamish was nearly enough to distract viewers from the slightly alarming development that Fremantle closed the lead to a mere 17 points with 13 minutes still to play.

Cue Buddy – a nice mark and goal. Phew!

Then the highlight of the match, and the only snippet likely to figure in footage shown on the "round by round" segment on Brownlow night: Luke Hodge, uncharacteristically indecisive, was caught by Hayden Ballantyne in the pocket, the ball spilled and Ballantyne, lying on the ground, got a neat handball over to Ryan Crowley, who was standing in the centre of the goals, pretty much on the goal line – at most he was 20 centimetres out. Crowley raised his boot to volley it through from mid-air, but somehow managed to hook it at such a severe angle that it hit the post! Perhaps he should have headed it.

Heartened by this fortuitous miss, Hawthorn slammed on three quick goals – two to Roughead and one to Breust – to close out the match by 42 points – coincidentally, the answer to the "meaning of life" in Douglas Adams's trilogy, *The Hitchhiker's Guide to the Galaxy*, proving that even in a seemingly innocuous match, Hawthorn operates at a level of cosmic significance.

Final scores: Hawthorn 18.10.118 d Fremantle 11.10.76

Ladder position: 4th

What we learned: Basil Zempilas is a leg man who likes his footballers neatly turned out.

What we already knew: Avoid Hoddle Street when there's a big game at the G. Actually, just avoid Hoddle Street.

THE TWILIGHT SAGA

ROUND 5 – HAWTHORN V NORTH MELBOURNE
MCG, Saturday 28 April 2013

It's a strange, eerie time, twilight; no longer daytime but not quite night, not yet dark but no longer light. It's a time when petals close and dew descends (not Stuart Dew either), the cold moon rises and the day's warmth ends, when wild birds squawk and the undead walk. It's an in-between time, an interval that opens a crack in the continuum, a crack through which evil sprites slip to weave their spells, and mystical spirits transform men into beasts, and vampires turn veins into drinking wells.

Whatever otherworldly events might hold sway at twilight, it's a timeslot that doesn't suit Hawthorn. Weird things happen at this hour, unexplained phenomena occur, and this Round 5 match was the living proof: ruckman Max Bailey was our most dangerous crumbing forward, snagging three early goals; Sam Mitchell couldn't get hold of the ball in the middle; Brent "Goo" Guerra repeatedly kicked the ball on the full; Luke Hodge seemed to vanish, or at least wasn't in the action; one of Luke Breust's kicks was "touched" retrospectively in a goal review; and Buddy dropped chest marks, spilled handballs and missed easy shots (okay, so not all that weird). In fact, Buddy had a rare goalless game.

Sure, we still won, but it was far from convincing and if not for Cyril, it might not have been a win at all. And even then, some evil twilight hex tore his hamstring and laid him low before the end.

Hawks fans will recall that the 2012 Preliminary Final against Adelaide, in which we struggled to assert our natural superiority and barely fell over the line, was also played at twilight.

But perhaps Hawthorn's difficulty at this particular hour of the day has less to do with the mystical nature of twilight, the moon rising and vampires stalking the earth, than it does with more mundane matters like "bodyclock" adjustment.

Is it perhaps that the game starts at the time it really should be ending? Are the players' bodies winding down naturally when we need them to be warming up? Is it that it's too late for an afternoon match and too early for a night match, leaving the players in a state of disequilibrium? I know I'm usually enjoying a quiet alcohol-fuelled snooze at about that time on a Sunday, so I can't blame the players if they're less than fully alert.

Or is it just that North Melbourne played pretty well for the majority of the match?

BLOOD-SUCKING VAMPIRES

I can't say I'm familiar with the synopsis of the *Twilight* series, having never read the books or watched the films. I do know, however, that the plot revolves around a trio of "old school" blood-sucking vampires, James, Victoria and Laurent, who come to town and lay waste to the community.

A trio of blood-sucking vampires ... hmm, sounds familiar ... perhaps something like Luke Farmer, Heath Ryan and Matt Stevic, the trio of field umpires officiating on the Sunday evening in question, who seemed determined to suck the life out of the match. They certainly seemed to be of some otherworldly genus.

One notable factor in the Hawks' victory this week was that, according to all the key statistical data, North Melbourne was by far the superior team, winning the inside 50 count 63 to 47, contested possessions 149 to 126, hit-outs 47 to 26, kicks 216 to 204 and hand-balls 134 to 126.

These figures alone would normally equate to a comfortable North victory, but another statistic revealed an even greater discrepancy between the two sides: free kicks. The free-kick count was 30 to 15 in favour of North – that's double the number of free kicks. Double! This included 10 in the final quarter alone, including a passage of four free kicks that took the ball from Hawthorn's forward line to North Melbourne's without any other type of intervening disposal, culminating in Lindsay Thomas kicking his final goal – his second at least from a free kick. It was great that Lindsay had corrected his kicking after the 2012 season; now we just needed the umpires to improve in equal measure and get better at spotting the difference between a player being pushed illegally in a contest and a player throwing himself forward to give the illusion of having been pushed. His diving technique had become so nuanced he was even starting to work a triple backflip with pike into some of them. And even Italian soccer teams had shown interest.

Despite these evil portents, good ultimately prevailed. Like the sun rising just in time to ward off a vampire, the siren sounded with the ball bobbling about in North's forward line, and Hawthorn held on to win by three points. And just as Edward and Bella thwarted James (Brayshaw?) and his evil coven in *Twilight*, Hawthorn thwarted North Melbourne in this twilight encounter.

BRIAN THE VAMPIRE PLAYER

We mostly view vampires as members of the evil undead stalking the earth in search of vulnerable prey. *Twilight,* however, showed us that there are also good, even exceedingly handsome, vampires, so long as they're played by Robert Pattinson. With Ryan Schoenmakers' tragic injury the previous week, Hawthorn introduced key recruit Brian Lake into the team to play his first game for the Hawks. Some may contend that Brian is no Robert Pattinson in the looks department, but with his dark eyes and features, his brooding demeanour, slick movie-star haircut and new svelte frame, he'd cut a dashing, vampiric figure in a cape.

In addition to the look, he has the air of an immortal. This is his second life, after all, having already transformed from Brian Harris to Brian Lake several years ago. And now he has come to Hawthorn after most people had given him up for dead at the Western Bulldogs. Plus he has taken the number 17 jumper – the very number worn by club legend and games record-holder Michael Tuck, who was still playing at age 38. Okay, so some way off the average age of a vampire, but still an eternity for an AFL player.

It all suggests to me that Brian Lake is set to be around for a while longer. And this, his first game for Hawthorn, backed up this thought. He played very well, spoiling opposition marks and taking some well-judged marks of his own. It was, in fact, a Lake intercept mark that set up the attack that resulted in Sam Mitchell kicking a goal to put us in front late in the game. Lake maintained his composure with the ball and worked well with Gibson, Goo and Birch. North's statistical dominance, particularly in the inside 50 count, actually highlighted how well Hawthorn's defence played.

THE THIRD THING

In an earlier chapter I revealed that I'd undergone a hernia operation. In the week leading up to this match I suffered terrible tooth pain that resulted in a trip to the dentist and the commencement of a root-canal procedure.

The experience of lying back in the dentist chair undergoing emergency root-canal surgery, with its drilling and scraping, its grating and grinding, was not unlike watching Hawthorn struggling to get the ball forward and maintain possession against North, with its fumbling and bungling, its botching and blundering. It was excruciating – the football, that is. At least the dentist administers an anaesthetic.

The best balm for any Hawthorn discomfort I was feeling was Cyril Rioli. His three scintillating third-quarter goals, plus another in the final quarter, had kept us in the match.

As we know, catastrophes and ill luck tend to run in threes, so after the hernia and the root canal, I'd been waiting for the third curse to strike, wondering what diabolical form it might take. And then it happened: with the Hawks trailing by two points, Jack Gunston put the ball out in front of Cyril Rioli, who was one-out with Shaun Atley on the wing, and as Cyril set off in pursuit of the ball his hamstring tore just as he got his boot to it. There it was: the third thing. Sure, it didn't happen to me, but this was even worse – it happened to Cyril.

With our indifferent form and Cyril's hamstring injury, Hawthorn's *Twilight* saga certainly belongs in the same horror genre as its literary equivalent. And just like the books, there's a series of sequels, as we play Adelaide at the same cursed time next week.

Final scores: Hawthorn 14.15.99 d North Melbourne 13.18.96
Ladder position: 4th
What we learned: North Melbourne selected Majak Daw for his second successive game, and there have been some promising signs that he'll become an exciting player. The first Sudanese-born man to play at AFL level, he began with a bang the previous week in his first match against Brisbane, taking a soaring

mark and kicking a goal in the first minute of the match. He then suffered a head clash and had to leave the field before the first quarter was over. He tested Hawthorn in this match, too, taking some good marks. If not for wayward kicking, he would have proven a very dangerous forward, but his first-quarter tackle on Shaun Burgoyne, while unwelcome from a Hawthorn perspective, was nonetheless spectacular.

What we already knew: Without Cyril, the Hawks might well have become the walking undead.

TRY AND BE NICE

On the eve of Round 6, Caroline Wilson reported in *The Age* an AFL proposal to enlist high-profile players to lead a campaign to stamp out abuse of opposition players at football matches. All very admirable and right up there with AFL campaigns to say no to racism, promote gender equality, tackle homophobia and resolve the civil war in Syria. Such is the scope and breadth of their extra-curricular interests and activities, it's easy to forget that the AFL is actually a sporting organisation rather than a government agency, left-wing think-tank or guild of ethicists.

Of course, announcing such a plan on the morning of the day Collingwood is set to take on a St Kilda side boasting the re-inclusion of Stephen Milne after he served a one-match suspension for clutching at the face of Essendon's Courtney Dempsey might be a little misguided. Collingwood fans and Milne have a long and proud tradition of mutual abuse. Not just the fans; even Mick Malthouse, when he was Collingwood coach, had a well-documented incident of abusing Milne, so it's asking a bit much of Collingwood fans to completely rewire their thinking overnight and give Milney an ovation as he comes off the bench. Especially when you consider that his nickname is "Tip-rat".

As it transpired, they didn't. Footage of Milne lining up a shot from the boundary line in the third quarter as the Saints challenged showed a female Collingwood fan – who looked a bit like Joffa's disgruntled sister – leaning over the fence waving a 'Go Pies' placard in his face and mouthing off in his ear. I can't lip-read but I suspect she wasn't enquiring after the health of his family or asking if he'd read any good books lately. I'd be impressed if Milney had read any books lately, let alone any good ones. In the end, he kicked out on the full.

REASONS TO HATE NORTH MELBOURNE

It was also concerning to hear reports of racial abuse at both the Collingwood v Essendon and Hawthorn v North Melbourne matches over the previous weekend. Some might argue that it's no surprise to learn that Collingwood fans were implicated. After all, they were behind one of the most well-known racial abuse incidents in AFL history. This year is the 20th anniversary of the famous Winmar jumper moment at Victoria Park. On that day in 1993, after defeating Collingwood at their home ground, St Kilda's indigenous champion Nicky Winmar lifted his jumper to show his bare skin to the Collingwood fans who had been racially abusing him during the match. He reportedly said, "I'm black and I'm proud to be black!"

It was a powerful gesture and became emblematic in the struggle for reconciliation in the AFL. But from that watershed moment, it is disturbing that some footy fans, and indeed the rest of us, haven't come very far.

It is distressing to hear that Hawthorn fans were also reported to have racially abused North players, presumably Majak Daw and Daniel Wells. I mean, North Melbourne is a perfectly nice team, and they played well in our match the previous weekend, but there are plenty of quite valid reasons to hate them, so it's disappointing that any of our number would resort to race.

Some opposition fans might hate North Melbourne because of Boomer Harvey, Wayne Carey or even James Brayshaw. Or all three. I hate North Melbourne for defeating Hawthorn in the 1975 Grand Final and 1977 Preliminary Final (no, I still haven't gotten over them), and more recently the 2007 semi-final. North Melbourne has an unhappy habit of defeating Hawthorn at key moments, surely the most heinous crime imaginable.

North offers a veritable cornucopia of loathing opportunities, so why would you need to target Majak Daw and Daniel Wells – two players who are among the most exciting in the competition to watch? Sure, Wells played annoyingly well against us, but that is because he's a great player in good form. As for Daw, give the guy a break; it was only his second game.

Besides, it defies logic that supporters of a team that relies on Buddy Franklin, Cyril Rioli, Shaun Burgoyne and Bradley Hill could muster a racial taunt without their internal hypocrite gauge causing their brains to explode. Between them, this quartet is probably responsible for over 80 per cent of Hawthorn's scoring opportunities. If the architects of the White Australia Policy were Hawthorn supporters, even they'd be on their feet cheering this fabulous foursome.

To their credit, Hawthorn players were certainly trying to get the message across. Caroline Wilson highlighted in her article that Hawthorn champ Brad Sewell, in one of his Fox Footy appearances, had spoken out against racial taunts directed at players, and also that injured team-mate Xavier Ellis had used Twitter to send a similar message to Hawks fans.

Of course, this raises the question of who is following Xavier Ellis on Twitter, and why. Who is so bereft of news input and commentary that they would need to follow Xavier Ellis, be it on Twitter or anywhere else? Don't get me wrong, I love the X-man. Perhaps no one loves him more, but as for wanting access to his every thought and philosophical speculation ... call me shallow, but I'll stick to following TAB.com.au's sports betting spokesperson, Jaimee Rogers, on Instagram.

What we learned: Well, not much, it seems. On the topic of being respectful to players and shunning racism, it's not quite time for Joffa to don his gold jacket and hold up his "Game Over" banner.

What we already knew: It will take more than the exhortations of Caroline Wilson and a few high-profile players for footy fans to be nice to Stephen Milne. And that includes St Kilda fans.

But it is not just Collingwood fans who can exhibit a nasty vitriolic streak. A casual glance through the readers' comments section of any website article, whether it be about football, American foreign policy or *Australia's Got Talent* contestants, reveals that the distance between blandishment and bile is short indeed, and that the human disposition is geared more towards venomous put-down than charitable platitude. In fact, the outer at the football is a veritable church group compared to online chat forums.

AAMI STADIUM CONDEMNED – UNFIT FOR HAWTHORN HABITATION

With Adelaide and Port Adelaide set to relocate their home games from AAMI Stadium to the Adelaide Oval from the 2014 season, this could well have been one of Hawthorn's final visits to a ground where we've only rarely enjoyed success – with our Round 16 game against Port later in the season to be our final match at the venue, barring finals.

I've never been to this ground, but I still won't miss it and I'm sure I speak for everyone at Hawthorn when I say that the move can't come soon enough. Besides, Adelaide Oval is so picturesque, as cricket commentators never tire of telling us, and I'm looking forward to heading over there in 2014 to catch a game.

It's well documented that Hawthorn has never played well at this venue, from our inauspicious debut in Round 1, 1991, when the newly minted Crows whipped us by 89 points, through numerous other humiliations over the past 22 years.

To be specific, the Hawks have lost on 19 occasions at AAMI Stadium and won just eight times prior to Saturday's match. There was a famous semi-final win against Port in 2001, a narrow win over the Crows in our premiership year of 2008, consecutive wins over

Port in 2011 and 2012 when the Power were barely competitive, and, well, only a handful of others.

It's hard to account for our problems in Adelaide – is it the ubiquitous churches distracting our boys with the call to religious devotion? Is it the award-winning wineries leading wine-buff Hawks to think about laying down reds rather than laying tackles? Is it the cultural distractions of a famous university town and arts-loving community? Or is it just that the use of this ground as an AFL venue has coincided with our least successful period since the '60s?

Despite this dark history, hopes were reasonably high for a victory in 2013, with the Hawks going well and the Crows having started slowly. It was also the 20th anniversary of a famous Hawks win at this ground in Round 6, 1993. On that occasion Jason Dunstall bagged nine goals, and while we couldn't look to target him one-out in the goal square this week, we had Buddy, and surely he couldn't go goal-less for the second consecutive week ... could he?

Of course, no Hawthorn fan is confident when our boys step onto the AAMI Stadium turf, and working against us this week were some compelling forces: the match was being played at AAMI Stadium; it was commencing at the spooky and cursed time of twilight; we were turned out in our all-white clash strip; Cyril was injured; Max Bailey, our three-goal hero from the previous week, was a late withdrawal; and, as it turned out, we were also virtually without Buddy, who again didn't kick a goal.

All bad portents, so our eventual triumph, although narrow, was all the more heroic for it.

HAWTHORN 2008 – THE PERFECT VINTAGE

We were back at Chan-Tha's place to view the match on Fox Footy. I upgraded my membership from bean bag to couch for this one, so I had a clear view of the action, plus table service when Chan-Tha brought out her mum's famous spring rolls. It was like being in the members'.

Since this was Adelaide, we thought about picking up a bottle of the newly released Penfolds Grange 2008 to quaff during the match. As a wine bottled in a Hawthorn premiership year, it reveals rich, nuanced flavours and boasts a complex nose, which roughly translates as the smell of success. The 2008 vintage is considered the perfect wine, which comes as no surprise to Hawks fans, as lots of things went right for us that year, but as it's priced at around $700 a bottle, we plumped instead for a six-pack of Little Creatures Bright Ale at around $4 a bottle. Not as complex – true – but also not as costly. And still a step above West End Bitter.

Fox Footy likes to have a legion of commentators and expert analysts in the box and ringing the boundary. Like a footy team packing the backline, Fox Footy crowds the box with a veritable throng, which on this occasion included Eddie McGuire, Anthony Hudson, Dermott Brereton, Mark Ricciuto, David King and possibly one or two others. Perhaps like the ABC's political coverage, Fox Footy's charter obliges them to give equal time to each side; hence, Dermie was there to provide an informed Hawthorn perspective and to offset Ricciuto's blatant Crows bias.

Alongside the great Dermie, however, was Eddie McGuire. I hadn't heard Eddie call a game since Channel 9 had the television rights, so it struck afresh just how irritating he can be. Overexcited over the incidental, he sees a melee in every jumper tug and a momentum shift with every goal. I could question the ethics of having a serving club president calling games, remembering that when the match-review committee sits down to view an incident, the voice they hear is that of the Collingwood president trying to heighten the drama of every scuffle and accidental collision. Or I could draw a connecting line between Eddie's regular pronouncements on how the AFL compromises the integrity of the competition through salary-cap inequality and the lack of goal-line technology, yet sees no apparent conflict of interest in the president of one club being the official broadcast voice of a game involving opposition teams. Or, worse, his own team. But I won't because, really, it's not that so much, it's more that he's just irritating to listen to.

In Round 2 Fox Footy introduced "Press Red for Ed", where Eddie provided a separate but completely biased call for Collingwood fans. This really is the perfect scenario, not only for Collingwood fans; they should do it every week so that you can watch Fox Footy safe in the knowledge that Eddie is marooned on an entirely different frequency.

IRONMAN 3

Call me naïve, but I went to see *Ironman 3* in the week leading up to this match assuming it was about Jordan Lewis, Hawthorn's own steel-armoured number 3. Jordan is, with the possible exception of Luke Hodge, the toughest player in the team (at least in his own mind). I proudly sport his number 3 on the back of my own Hawthorn jumper. Admittedly, I bought the jumper from the heritage range and the number 3 was already there in honour of the greatest "3" of them all, Leigh Matthews. But Jordan Lewis more than lives up to his famous forebear. His performance against Collingwood in the 2011 Preliminary Final, when he almost single-handedly willed us into the Grand Final, ranks as one of the most determined and courageous games I've ever seen by a Hawthorn player. I tear up just thinking about it. And I don't mind admitting I've had a bit of a man-crush on him ever since.

Obviously, I was disappointed to discover my mistake when the film commenced and instead of Jordan Lewis I found myself watching a sort of wannabe robot, though at least Gwyneth Paltrow was flitting in and out. Yet there are echoes of the movie in the way this Round 6 match unfolded.

The narrative arc of super-hero movies follows a fairly standard template. Early on you establish the identity of the heroes and the baddies; the hero will be wisecracking his way through an untroubled, uber-cool lifestyle, probably with water views and a beautiful companion, while the bad guy will be unassuming, perhaps grossly and distinctively deformed in some way, but industriously going about his evil ways.

In setting the scene, you should show an environment in which life is unruffled and everything runs smoothly. Then you shatter that tranquillity with a violent and disruptive criminal act by the baddies. A battle ensues. The baddies establish an ascendency and land a seemingly killer blow, leaving no realistic chance of escape or redemption for the hero, who has quite likely been severely debilitated or sustained a critical injury. Then, drawing on some special power or resolve, or receiving assistance from an unlikely source, the hero fights back, gains the upper hand and, despite a flicker of a revival for the evildoer, ultimately prevails.

Certainly that's the template that *Ironman 3* followed, and it also describes the pattern of the Adelaide v Hawthorn match.

The first quarter opened in an idyllic land where the sun shone, daffodils bloomed, children squealed with delight, kittens and fluffy bunnies romped, and Bradley Hill skipped freely down the wing to kick a couple of goals.

Our first goal, in fact, came from Ironman Lewis, then Hodge squeezed one through after a strong mark and even the Poo got on the end of one. Five goals to one in the opening quarter and the good guys had established their place in happy land.

When Michael Osborne added another in the first minute of the second quarter, the storyline looked like it might develop into the Disney version of a fairy tale. But then the evildoers struck, taking over the narrative and terrorising our happy land by controlling general play and kicking four unanswered goals. Our debilitated and struggling heroes were out of energy and ideas, and barely hanging on by two points at half time.

An even third quarter saw the Hawks regain some of their powers, with two goals to Jack Gunston and one to Isaac Smith, but then Adelaide laid us low with two late goals to Sam Jacobs and Richard Douglas, leaving the Hawks gasping for life with a five-point three-quarter-time lead. By this stage Patrick Dangerfield was completely dominating the midfield and tearing the Hawks apart, just as he had done in the previous year's Preliminary Final, when he continually won the ball and got it moving forward in the general direction of danger forward Kurt Tippett. His performance in that match was every bit as powerful as Jordan Lewis's in the 2011 Preliminary Final. It's perhaps significant that Dangerfield wears number 32 (23 backwards), and under any other circumstance – that is, against any other opponent – I love watching him play, but this was not the time for him to be turning it on. Comfy as Chan-Tha's couch is, we were beginning to squirm in our seats.

When Scott Thompson goaled three minutes into the final term to put the Crows in front, it looked like curtains for our heroic Hawks, with the hometown crowd baying for the Crows to finish us off. But then, as is the way with such narratives, we received help from an unlikely source. As Thompson marked within range, the umpire paid a free kick against him for a push on Hawthorn's David Hale. It was more of a brush, really, or a caress, but it was Umpire Appreciation Week and we certainly appreciated this thoughtful gesture. From the ensuing 50-metre penalty for abuse – don't you love the way a bad decision is often compounded? – Hale got it forward and Jarryd Roughead soccered through a goal to re-establish our lead. Shouts of "Rough!" echoed through Richmond.

As is usually the way with such stories, the heroes mustered one last herculean effort, with Hodge, Mitchell, Burgoyne, Roughead, Sewell and Gibson coming to the rescue, and Breust went on to deliver the killer blows by bursting through packs to bang home two decisive goals in a minute – a brace that provoked high-fives all round and the now traditional Gregorian intoning of "Breuuuust" from Oscar and me. This was followed by Rough creating an interception and getting it forward, where Gunston marked strongly and goaled. After the exhilaration of Breust's two goals, this was the goal that allowed us to relax, clink some celebratory Bright Ales (or Sprite, in Oscar's case) and start composing cocky tweets.

Sure, there was the usual last-gasp flicker from the baddie as Scott Thompson and Sam Kerridge added late goals for the Crows, but this was like wounded henchmen regaining consciousness just sufficiently to grab their guns and fire off some random shots. These amounted to nothing but a flesh wound and the good guys prevailed, the stirring theme music swelled in the theatre and we all went home happy that justice had been served.

Actually, it was Saturday night by the time the match ended so we didn't go home immediately. As with any close match, you have to take a moment to gather your thoughts and relive the decisive incidents, or at least finish the snacks.

And, as in a traditional movie postscript, the hero got the girl. The day after the match Cyril tweeted news of his engagement.

Despite our historical woes at AAMI Stadium, we'd now won our last three there. Perhaps they shouldn't move to the Adelaide Oval, after all.

Final scores: Hawthorn 13.11.89 d Adelaide 11.12.78
Ladder position: 5th

What we learned: If not for the risk of an ankle injury, Luke Breust should get into roller derby. The first of his final-quarter goals came straight from the roller-derby playbook: Sewell delivered high to the goal square, Breust flew from behind but couldn't quite bring down the mark; however, he kept control of the ball when it hit the ground, put his head down and burst through a pack of three Crows plus Burgoyne in a style reminiscent of Skate Bush from The Dolls of Hazard racking up the points in a derby jam. And then he banged it home.

   This was, in fact, the 23rd year of matches at AAMI stadium – there's that number again – so it was no wonder we triumphed.

What we already knew: That the fixture (or "fix", as Hawthorn fans refer to it) requiring us to play all of 2012's finalists in the first seven weeks of the season would be tough – so at 5–1 with just Sydney to come, we were doing well. Some big wins and some close ones – and not necessarily the ones we might have thought. But 6–1 or 5–2 after the next match would put us in a good position.

   The free kick against Thompson was the wrong call, but only if you look at it in a narrow football sense. If you look at it from a utilitarian perspective, where the consequence of a given action is the only test of whether it is the right thing to do, then the outcome – a Hawthorn victory – completely justified it.

   Besides, everyone was going on about this free kick without any forensic examination of some of the howlers awarded to Adelaide in front of goal. In the first quarter Dangerfield scored after a very dodgy free, Vince got one in the second quarter, and in the final quarter Bradley Hill was penalised for deliberate out of bounds after being pushed over the boundary line.

Given that it's Umpire Appreciation Week, however, we just had to be big enough to let those go.

Apropos of nothing: The TV guide in *The Age* on the Monday following the match listed for Channel 9 at 9.30: "*Footy Classified* (includes *Crimestoppers*)" – presumably this refers to the now weekly segment on Essendon.

ESSENDON – CAUGHT IN POSSESSION

BETWEEN THE ROUNDS
5–10 May 2013

There was a weird internal dichotomy at play when I lay down to sleep at night. Two opposing forces were battling for control of my mind. On the one hand, concern over whether Buddy would stay at Hawthorn was keeping me awake at nights with fretting and heavy sweats, but countering this was another issue lulling me gently with the sleep of the just – Essendon's drug scandal. As far as karma goes, or comeuppance, or just good old-fashioned spite, you couldn't beat a scandal that threatened to rid us of Essendon for good.

From the time the story of Essendon's supplements program broke on the eve of the 2013 season, every journalist, past player, shock jock and lobbyist has had their say. Some have advocated the immediate sacking of the board, coaching staff and WAGs; others have demanded that Essendon be banned from playing, or at least banned from breeding any more Danihers. And then there are some who are just glad there's a topic other than gay marriage to discuss on *Q&A*. With each new revelation, more voices joined the chorus. *The Age* on Tuesday 7 May carried eight separate articles about the crisis at Essendon. And then there was the *Herald-Sun*, *The Australian* and the 15 to 20 footy shows on TV that raked over the same old ground nightly.

And just to round it off, in the *Herald-Sun* on Wednesday 8 May, Jeff Kennett had his say, arguing, rather predictably, that heads should have already rolled at Essendon. Who would have thought he'd have a viewpoint?

Despite this, the definitive view has yet to be expressed, so it's time this story was told the way it should have been – that is, from the Hawthorn perspective.

If you listened to any Essendon supporter talk about this topic (if you couldn't avoid it, that is), they would've had you believe that *The Age*'s chief football writer, Caroline Wilson, was the chief culprit in the drug scandal enveloping their club. "She had it in for Hirdy," they'd tell you. "It was a witch hunt," they'd assert.

They could have also picked on *The Australian*'s football writer Patrick Smith, who was equally condemnatory of the culture at Essendon, but as no one reads *The Australian* he escaped such censorious name-calling. As well, I suspect it was just easier to pick on a woman.

At some point when listening to these diatribes, I liked to point out that Caroline Wilson hadn't injected anyone with pig's blood or goat's placenta, forced anyone to snort smegma or put anyone on a drip of rattlesnake semen. She'd merely reported on events, and right from the time the story broke she'd adopted the line that it was a duty-of-care issue and that the players needed to be protected. To date, she hasn't been proven to have exaggerated. To blame her for Essendon's "pharmalogically experimental environment", to use Ziggy Switkowski's phrase, was akin to blaming Bob Woodward and Carl Bernstein for exposing Nixon's duplicities, rather than, say, blaming Nixon.

To restate it, Caroline Wilson didn't inject anyone or introduce a controversial supplements program at Essendon or anywhere else, and while a prudent and careful observer may exercise caution in jumping to conclusions, I submit that, being a Hawthorn fan, I am obliged by the forces of history, by the very genetic instructions encrypted into my

DNA, to assume Essendon to be guilty of all allegations levelled against them, regardless of how ill-founded or unproven.

Some fence-sitting, wuss-bag commentators – usually ex-players or known Essendon fans – said that we needed to wait for the investigation to be completed and for the facts to emerge before we came to conclusions, judged and condemned. Where was the fun in that? Besides, this uncharacteristic measured response from footy commentators was at odds with the normal hair-trigger reactions they exhibited over other moral issues that had filtered into the footy world, such as Ben Cousins's tribulations or Wayne Carey's marital problems.

Hawthorn fans didn't need to wait for pathology results or compare interview accounts to come to our own conclusions about what took place. Essendon was a club, after all, which had already been found guilty of salary-cap rorting in the '90s – and, worse, had defeated Hawthorn in successive Grand Finals in 1984–85.

Hird himself had been accused in some sections of the media of taking anti-ageing supplements. These accusations, I suspect, weren't based on toxicology analysis of hair samples or white cell counts in blood tests, but simple envy at his enduring youthful good looks.

"THE PILLS WON'T HELP YOU NOW"
– THE CHEMICAL BROTHERS

One of the aspects of this story I found entertaining was to read football journalists wrestling with new concepts and contexts. Just as the Wayne Carey/Kelli Stevens scandal gave the word "bathroom" unlikely prominence in the football lexicon, journalists were now peppering their articles with "peptides" instead of "possessions", "calf colostrum" instead of "calf complaints" and "Switkowski" instead of "Sierakowski".

Much was anticipated of Ziggy Switkowski's report on the

internal governance and medical practices at Essendon during 2012. Why, I can't imagine. Two of the most pivotal players in the saga, Dean "The Weapon" Robinson, Essendon's high-performance manager, and Stephen "The Pharmacist" Dank, a sports scientist, weren't even interviewed for the report. It was difficult, therefore, to see what concrete findings it could possibly reach. It was like trying to measure global warming without checking the temperature. The report may as well have been prepared by Ziggy Stardust.

With the media bandying about characters with nicknames such as "The Weapon" and "The Pharmacist", and introducing a bio-chemist known as "Dr Ageless", who was also alleged to be mixed up in it all, this trio sounded less like a football club's support crew and more like baddies from a Batman movie.

"THE DRUGS DON'T WORK" – THE VERVE

Despite this issue surfacing in February, here we were in May and ASADA still hadn't interviewed any of the players. I know, they'd been busy with NRL club Cronulla, which was being investigated over similar allegations, but this had all started 10 weeks ago. Meanwhile, Essendon was winning games of football.

While I was keen for the investigation to interrupt Essendon's season, the more games Essendon won, the more we'd all be able to enjoy it when half the team was suspended and their points were wiped later in the year.

Which led us to the serious issue of what, if any, sanctions Essendon should face? Ben Cousins was banned for 12 months for bringing the game into disrepute, even though he never failed a drug test. Nor was he ever even alleged to have taken performance-enhancing substances – just good-time, albeit illegal, recreational drugs. So, given this precedent, you'd have to assume severe penalties would be meted out: the coaching panel banned, players suspended or banished to play for Melbourne, all their points wiped, premierships stripped from them, and all coaching staff and officials sent to Manus Island.

As for individuals, Jobe Watson's 2012 Brownlow might well be ripped from his neck and awarded to Hawthorn's Sam Mitchell and Richmond's Trent Cotchin, who finished equal second that year. Perhaps there could be a ceremony where Jobe presented both Sam and Trent with the 2012 Brownlow. His dad, Tim, could bring it to us live on Channel 7.

"THE NEEDLE AND THE DAMAGE DONE" – NEIL YOUNG

Much was being made of Dr Bruce Reid's opposition to the controversial supplements regime and the "missing letter" in which he detailed his concerns to the coaching panel. This issue was perhaps easier to understand when you considered Dr Reid's advanced age and how long he had been serving at Essendon. Firstly, would anyone at Essendon have known what a letter was? He should have tweeted his disquiet over the exact contents of the compounds being given to players. Or posted on Facebook. Someone might have taken notice then.

Also, Dr Reid had been club doctor at Essendon for so long that when he started there, sometime in the eighteenth or nineteenth century, it was common practice to use leeches to suppress fevers and purify blood. Leeches, cow's placenta – doesn't sound like medicine has advanced that much, really.

Essendon fans would strenuously deny that there was any evidence their club had done anything wrong and point out that no players had tested positive for banned substances. They would then dispute any suggestion of proposed penalties or sanctions against the club and question how many other clubs were running similar programs. As if that made it okay! That was akin to the conservative view on climate change: that Australia doesn't need to take action because China isn't.

The question Essendon fans *should* have been asking, which was exactly the point Caroline Wilson made, was that if the allegations were true, why had the club persisted on a pathway that put its own beloved players at risk, and which would make any successes devoid of honour?

"BORNE BACK CEASELESSLY INTO THE PAST"
F. SCOTT FITZGERALD, *THE GREAT GATSBY*

ROUND 7 – HAWTHORN V SYDNEY
MCG, Saturday 11 May 2013

For the next few years at least, all Hawthorn v Sydney matches will be imbued with the events of Grand Final Day 2012; each meeting of the two teams will carry an echo of what transpired on that day. Particularly this, the first one. If the Swans defeated us, we'd acknowledge that we'd been beaten by a superior team and even take some solace in the fact that the 2012 Grand Final result was perhaps a just one. If we defeated the Swans, however, the victory would be laced with a melancholic note of the more important victory we couldn't achieve – we'd catch an agonising peek of the paradise in which we might have lolled. Within our small triumph we'd glimpse our greater failure, and our celebrations would be somewhat tempered as a result.

The match was marketed as the Grand Final rematch, but it was only a rematch for the vanquished; only they had anything to prove. As Howard Jacobson writes in his satire of the publishing world *Zoo Time*, "Success is arbitrary and wayward; only failure is the real measure of things."

Unlike Grand Final week, this time there was no forensic scrutiny of ins and outs or individual player fitness, no parading of past champions or misty-eyed predictions carrying emotional resonance. In fact, the game nearly passed by unnoticed, given the hysteria surrounding the previous night's game between undefeated teams Geelong and Essendon. In successive nights, footy fans could watch the two best teams of 2013 and the two best teams of 2012.

What talk there was focused as much on Buddy's travails rather than any other aspect of the clash. The real problem with the pre-match build-up was not the constant references to Buddy being held goal-less for two consecutive weeks for the first time since 2005, a stat everyone learned and then felt the need to trot out, but that we had to endure an entire week of seeing super-slo-mo footage of Malceski kicking the match-sealing goal from 2012. As if it wasn't bad enough in real time.

Recovering from major surgery on the eve of the season, my Hawk buddy Chan-Tha was lying in her hospital bed when the TV fixed in her line of vision began showing a replay of the 2012 Grand Final – the whole match! With one hand she began to frantically ring the nurse's alarm, while with the other she no less frantically began to self-administer dosages of morphine from her dispenser. A panicked nurse appeared, imagining some desperate post-operative emergency, only to be confronted by a groggy Chan-Tha asking for the channel to be changed.

"Don't you like football?" the nurse enquired.

"Yes, but I support Hawthorn. I don't want to watch this."

The poor girl; her health was precarious enough without being subjected to that horror.

WHO'S THAT MOFO?

There had been talk pre-season that the AFL might use a Hawthorn v Sydney clash as part of a showcase to stamp out anti-homophobic attitudes and celebrate inclusiveness across sport and society.

It was easy to see why the Swans might be used as a vehicle for such a game, given the large gay population in Sydney. It was less clear, however, why Hawthorn would be involved, unless it was our all-white clash strip – featuring a jumper with a fluffy plumed hawk sitting pertly on the chest, white shorts and socks with brown, gold and white hoops – a combination that wouldn't look at all out of place on a Mardi-Gras float.

I wasn't sure if that idea was still on the agenda, but there was a hint of it pre-game. Instead of the usual footy fan in stonewash denim, trainers and ill-fitting track top, the coin toss was conducted by one of the most exotic creatures to set foot on the MCG since Madonna played there in the mid-'90s wearing her cone bra.

Draped in a patterned cloak, she wore a crimson head-dress with strings of beads dangling like a cork hat. It had perhaps once served as a lamp shade in a brothel. Ah, I thought, this must be a drag diva dressed as Gloria Swanson playing Norma Desmond from *Sunset Boulevard*, here to encourage harmony between people of different sexual orientations. It turned out the coin tosser was dressed this way as part a promotion for Dark MOFO – a music and arts festival being held at Hobart's MONA Gallery.

Using a football match as a marketing vehicle for a contemporary arts festival was perhaps even more baffling than using it as a vehicle to stamp out homophobia. I suspected even the most homophobic in the crowd would find the idea of sexual relations between two grunting, lubed-up footballers to be less confronting than some of the music and art they might experience at Dark MOFO.

BUDDY'S BACK

There was an even stranger presence than Dark MOFO in the centre square moments later, when the Poo lined up there for the first bounce. Clearly, it was one of Clarko's strategies to mess with Sydney's minds by putting the Poo in the middle at the start instead of, say, Hodge, Sewell or Burgoyne – just to name a few of the elite midfielders he could have called on.

Had Clarko assigned Brian Lake to join the Poo at the bounce, we might have boasted a midfield of equal potency to the sadly all-too-brief political alliance of Clive Palmer and Peter Slipper. Talk about a political dream team. Add Bob Katter, Barnaby Joyce and Cory Bernadi and you'd have had a political group as wacky as Sydney's midfield of Josh Kennedy, Kieren Jack, Daniel Hanneberry, Adam Goodes and Ryan O'Keefe was potent.

The pre-match babble about Buddy was quickly quietened when our man slotted his first goal just a few minutes in – and what a goal! Taking a mark on the flank outside 50, he turned boundary-side to get past Ted Richards, and on the run on his left side threaded a trademark Buddy special. After Gunston snapped a nice round-the-corner goal, Buddy then got front and centre to grab the ball from a Bailey spoil and slotted his second in five minutes. Bailey and Breust added two more and we had a handsome five-goals-to-one first quarter.

GOLDEN ROUGH

The blitz continued in the second quarter, led by Rough, who bagged three beauties. His first came from a set shot after taking a towering grab. His next goal came after Jordan Lewis tackled and dispossessed Adam Goodes. As Lewis tumbled over onto his back, he gave the ball a little kick and Rough plucked it from the boot and banged it home. The third came after a pass from the Poo, which the umpire deemed not to have travelled 15 metres, so Rough simply wheeled around and sent another one through. Rough was also responsible for one of Gunston's goals, pushing through a pack and getting a long handball to "the Gun", who had enough space to steady and steer home his second.

Buddy kicked another classic after fending off two defenders and slamming it round his body for his third.

But perhaps the best goal of the quarter came from Burgoyne: taking it straight from the bounce, he ran eight, possibly nine steps and rammed it home! What a goal! ... What? ... You can't be serious! "Too far," the umpire signalled in a trademark example of a delusional umpire who thinks 57,000 people turned up to watch him officiate the match rather than watch the champions play it.

ALL HAIL ... UH, HALE

A seven-goal half-time lead was surely going to be sufficient, and that seemed to be how the players approached it. The third quarter was uneventful, or perhaps it just seemed that way, given that I was drinking a pint in the Bullring Bar for most of it and could only see the action on a television monitor. It had taken so long to get served in the half-time rush that by the time I took my first sip, the players were back on the ground.

As we stood about watching the match on the screen, Chan-Tha pointed out Mark Williams also enjoying a drink in the Bullring; that's Mark Williams the 2008 Hawthorn premiership hero, not Mark Williams, or "Choco", the maverick Port Adelaide premiership coach.

On the screen I saw McGlynn start to get into the match. I almost felt sorry for Ben McGlynn. Almost but not quite. I would have felt sorry for him if he'd left Hawthorn for any other team. I'd always liked him at the Hawks. He was injured throughout 2008 when he was at Hawthorn, missing out on playing in our premiership, and then, having established himself as an important player for Sydney, he was injured in the 2012 finals and missed out on their premiership. As I said, I almost felt sorry for him.

There was a memorable passage of play from the Poo in the third quarter; using strength to wrestle the ball out of the centre to win a clearance, he then completely duffed the kick. He followed up to make amends, again stole the ball, and then again duffed the kick. Two superb acts and two clangers, all in the space of 30 seconds – that's why we love the Poo. As my friend Pete observed, "The problem with the Poo is that sometimes he thinks he's a good player."

In other words, he sees Cyril and Buddy perform these magical on-field feats and feels encouraged to try his own hand, without realising that not just any player can pull off those moves. The Poo is a tough, determined player, but he's a mere mortal compared to such deities as Cyril and Buddy.

Hawthorn forwards were taking it in turns to dominate: Buddy in the first; Rough and Gunston in the second; now it was Hale's turn in the third as he kicked a couple of important goals in quick succession to ensure that we maintained our advantage.

WHAT WE CAN LEARN FROM JAPANESE PORN?

Hale also got the first of the final quarter, but, despite this, Sydney continued to close on us. So Lewis's excellent snap to restore our superiority was most welcome. Here again, though, the umpires sought to wrest attention away from the players and onto themselves. After the goal umpire awarded a goal, a boundary umpire protested that the ball might have been touched. So up it went for review, where, naturally, the footage proved inconclusive for the simple reason that blurred footage will always be inconclusive. It's the same in cricket when they try to use video to determine if a ball was caught cleanly – it can never capture it. But instead of then taking the goal umpire's initial call – he had, after all, signalled a goal instantly and was in the perfect position – the field umpire took the word of the boundary umpire. The ensuing and quite resounding "Bullshit" chant was something Hawthorn supporters could be very proud of.

There must be something wrong with the cameras or the quality of the production at Australian sporting grounds. You can never pinpoint the precise moment the ball is touched or whether it grazes the post, yet in almost any half-decent Japanese porn movie you can pause it at any moment and see with absolute clarity which fingertip is grazing against which erogenous zone and whose incisor left bite marks on what thigh. If only the AFL could call on the resources and production standards of the pornography industry to fix the goal-review system.

The week before, an overly zealous umpire had helped the Hawks get over the line when he paid a free kick against Scott Thompson for a push-out in a marking contest. From the resulting free kick and 50-metre penalty to David Hale, Hawthorn stormed forward and kicked a goal to regain the lead. This week, overly zealous umpiring stripped Hawthorn of two goals – both of them sensational – turning a handsome eight-goal thumping of the Swans to a slightly less emphatic six-goal victory.

ORGIASTIC FUTURE

After his initial flourish, Buddy had been rather subdued. His only shot at goal in the second half was an inexplicable miss from about two metres – after which Sydney went forward and scored, reducing the margin to 25 points. Happily, Osborne and Burgoyne added two more to restore a decent margin and calm any emerging anxiety.

This was a great performance by the Hawks: Hodge, Roughead and Gibson were best afield, but every player contributed, metaphorically touching our erogenous zones one way or another.

If Hawthorn v Sydney matches must be viewed through the prism of the 2012 Grand Final, we could at least take some satisfaction in reversing that result on this occasion.

On the eve of Baz Luhrmann's film version of *The Great Gatsby* opening in Australia, I was reminded of Nick Carraway's observations at the very end of the novel. Referring to Gatsby's belief in "the orgiastic future", he says, "It eluded us then, but that's no matter – tomorrow we will run faster, stretch out our arms farther ... And one fine morning –"

He could have been referring to Hawthorn as much as Gatsby, and just as in the novel, Hawthorn's premiership parties will be every bit as "gleaming" and "dazzling" as Gatsby's famed soirees when we win this year's flag. Did someone say "orgiastic future"? Bring on September!

Final scores: Hawthorn 18.11.119 d Sydney Swans 12.10.82
Ladder position: 3rd
What we learned: There was a person called Darrin Baxter who once played for Hawthorn. The scarf minding the seat in front of me was festooned with a number of classic Hawthorn heritage pins and the best collection I've seen of player badges for obscure Hawthorn alumni. Not for this supporter the staid old names of Peter Knights, Leigh Matthews or Jason Dunstall. Whoever owned this scarf preferred the likes of Darrin Baxter, Justin Crawford and Paul Cooper. I remember Paul Cooper and Justin Crawford playing. Justin Crawford wore number 23 and was nicknamed Joan to distinguish him from his more celebrated brother Shane, who of course was known as Cindy. I can honestly say, however, that I have no memory of Darrin Baxter playing, though a quick internet search shows that he played 27 games for Hawthorn in 1993–94, including an Elimination Final.

I have a Simon Crawshay badge that would fit in nicely on that scarf. Crawshay, who also wore number 23, played just 19 games in 1994–96. My favourite obscure Hawthorn players, however, are Michael Zemski, who wore number 10 and played just eight games in 1973–74, but sported an impressive John Platten-like hair-do; and someone called Andrew Demetriou, who wore number 36 and played just three games in 1988.

What we already knew: In a post-match interview, Roughead referred to his level of fitness as akin to an "asthmatic turtle". I'm not sure how accurate that is, but the comment showed that he is as adept with metaphor as he is with a Sherrin from outside 50. This was another great display of his strength and insouciance.

Elsewhere: It was a surprise later that night when Wigan defeated Manchester City to win the FA Cup, but an even bigger surprise was that it took nearly a whole minute of the preamble before Les Murray used the phrase "David and Goliath battle" when referring to the respective teams.

LET'S GET HIGH ON HAWTHORN

Like most Hawthorn fans, I approached this match against the newest AFL franchise like an addict anticipating a good binge, the equivalent of the transition from sipping a vodka, lime and soda to vodka eyeballing. I was after an immediate and intense rush; I wanted a glut of goals. And while we kicked the first five goals and five of the last six, for the middle part of the match we were, by comparison, like a recovering heroin addict on the methadone program, getting our fix in small doses.

Of course, I draw this analogy on the back of news that there'd been a sharp increase in AFL players testing positive to illicit drugs – the fun ones, that is, not the illicit ones that can potentially make you better at football. No one had tested positive to those, so therefore there's no reason to suspect anyone was, or is, taking them.

The report released by the AFL revealed that cocaine is the recreational drug of choice among AFL players, which really just tells us they get paid too much. Cocaine reportedly provides the user with an increased sense of energy and alertness, a heightened mood and a feeling of supremacy. On the other hand, it also increases irritability, paranoia, restlessness and anxiety. Most footy fans would find these differing moods and emotional states readily familiar just through following their team from week to week – in some cases, just through following them during the same quarter.

As I joined Chan-Tha and Pete to take in our match from Launceston against the fledgling Giants, I was hoping for an experience at the heady-rush end of the scale, and at the very least a relaxed, anxiety-free game. Nevertheless, we eschewed illicit drugs in favour of a rich, strong Hawthorn Amber Ale.

HAWTHORN – MY DRUG OF CHOICE

There was an initial rush of sorts. Once Buddy passed to Rough for the first goal, three more followed quickly from Liam Shiels, Hodge and Burgoyne, before Rhys Palmer juggled a mark and got one back for the Giants. Palmer was sporting what Chan-Tha described as a European headband, a thin spaghetti strap around his head, except, as she pointed out, he wore it in such a way that it actually trapped the hair in his eyes.

The highlight of the first quarter came from Mitchell, of course: running on to a Gunston pass in the pocket, he looked for options inboard, but finding none, shrugged his shoulders and bent it through himself.

Facing an inexperienced opposition, Hawthorn took the opportunity to give former Cat Jonathan Simpkin his first full game, and former Eagle and Swan Matthew Spangher his debut for the Hawks. Spangher clearly has an avian bias – and, if his hairstyle and beard combo is any indication, something of a Jesus complex as well. But we didn't need miracles in this match. Buddy snagged a couple in the second quarter, the second of which was a strong snap after taking a handball from Burgoyne and bursting though a pack to goal.

But the Giants played quite well in the second quarter, and even though the Hawks were still in the ascendant, with Gunston kicking a couple and Rough adding his third, the Giants evened things up in the third and were even on top for parts of the quarter.

Over the middle period of the match, the Hawks kicked 9.9 to the Giants' 6.1, so while we were not exactly threatened, it wasn't the goal binge we were hoping for. In fact, for parts of the third quarter I felt like I was going cold turkey. Happily, a duffed clearance from GWS landed with Rough about 25 metres out, and just on the siren David Hale got on the end of one to restore a healthy buffer.

Halfway through the third quarter, and apropos of nothing in particular, the Fox Footy commentary team of Anthony Hudson, Brad Johnson, Tony Shaw, David King and Ben Dixon (there may well have been others) pondered the optimum time for Hawthorn to introduce its sub into the match. They then began to opine about which player Hawthorn might be taken off to facilitate the Poo's injection into the fray. Surprisingly, perhaps, they settled on Sam Mitchell on the basis that he had probably already secured the three Brownlow medal votes. Following this line of reasoning further, one of them suggested that subbing Mitchell off would, in fact, be proof that he already had the three Brownlow votes.

This raised several questions – chief among them being why would we ever sub Sam Mitchell off while he was still conscious, but also, should the coaching panel really be basing their decision on the likelihood or otherwise of Brownlow voting? And if so, would it not have made more sense to sub off someone playing poorly, someone who was unlikely to figure in the votes, and keep the good performers on the field? Even if the coaching panel was going to rest the good players without putting Brownlow votes at risk, this presupposes they had some insight into the vagaries of Brownlow voting, when really, the very fact that Sam Mitchell hadn't already won at least one Brownlow Medal exposed a gaping flaw in the system and rendered useless the idea of trying to second-guess it.

"JA, HELLO, MALMÖ. AMAAAZING SHOW!
OUR MAXIMUM POINTS GO TO HAWTHORN"

As it happened, the only voting system more flawed than the Brownlow, and only slightly less boring to watch, was also taking place over the same weekend. I refer of course to Eurovision. One of the only real differences between the two events is that the Brownlow isn't preceded by a four-hour production of over-the-top, high-camp pop songs performed by a succession of ludicrously costumed vocalists. Perhaps it would be better if it was.

The other difference between the two events is that participants in Eurovison squeal and wave team flags every time they get a vote, whereas AFL players shrug their shoulders dismissively, take a sip of their Crowny and shake their heads to convey that there must have been some regrettable mistake.

Wouldn't the Brownlow be better with a little less macho modesty and a bit more high-fiving, whoop-whooping, "I'm da man ... I'm gonna take you down!"-type antics from the boys?

The AFL could certainly learn a few lessons from the production of Eurovision. Instead of Andrew Demetriou intoning the 'one vote, two votes, three votes' mantra, they could adopt a similar system to Eurovision, with the umpires appearing by video link to announce their votes. They could film a selfie video in their dressing room after each match and then show it on the night. And Bruce McAvaney could sit centre stage like Petra Mede from host nation Sweden, receiving the votes while wearing a long, layered white gown and looking like a figurine on a wedding cake. A few lesbian-kissing scenes à la Finland's entry might also enliven the night.

HAWKS ON TOP!

The Hawks extended the healthy buffer in the final quarter with five goals to one, including Lewis intercepting a kick-in and Sewell fending off a couple of players to put one through. Even the Poo steered one through; he'd come on for Osborne in the third. The Hawthorn brains trust had evidently ignored the advice of the commentary team, taking off Osborne, who hadn't exactly given the stats person RSI, and leaving Mitchell out there to rack up Brownlow votes, unless of course the runner just got the blond hair confused and took off Osborne by mistake.

Rough polished the win by adding his fifth after the siren. Not necessarily the most exciting post-siren goal of the weekend – perhaps Nic Naitanui's match-winner for the Eagles against North had the edge there. With just a split-second remaining in the match, he flew above the pack of players to take a spectacular mark, then calmly slotted the goal to put the Eagles in front. As it happens, the Fox Footy boundary rider at our match was Ben Dixon, kicker of one of our most famous post-siren goals against Carlton in 2001.

In the end an 83-point victory gave us a nice, soothing high that allowed us to drift gently into the evening. When Collingwood defeated Geelong later that night we could lie back and luxuriate in top spot on the ladder for the first time in the season.

Eurovision 2013's winning song, "Only Teardrops" by Emmelie de Forest of Denmark, contains a refrain about how many times we can win and lose, a clear reference to win–loss ratio. And after this latest win over GWS, our win–loss ratio was a very healthy 7–1. So it may seem peevish to have been slightly dissatisfied with an 83-point victory, but the last time we'd played the Giants we'd won by 162 points – that's a 79-point turnaround! A repeat of that next time and we would be down to a match decided by a kick.

Final scores: Hawthorn 21.14.140 d Greater Western Sydney 9.3.57

Ladder position: 1st

What we learned: Jonathan Simpkin played well in his first full
game for the Hawks, as did Matt Spangher, who would do well
to either cut his hair to fit the neat Hawthorn look or turn his
patchy scrub of a beard into designer stubble and add a touch
of product. He could then go for the Italian soccer star or pimp
look.

What we already knew: The Hawthorn Amber Ale, a rich dark
ale, is just perfect for cold winter days watching the Hawks
play in Launceston.

NEARLY BLINDED BY THE SUNS

ROUND 9 – HAWTHORN V GOLD COAST
MCG, Sunday 26 May 2013

As much as I love the Hawks, I can't get to every match. Besides, I have other obsessions to indulge (so as not to incriminate myself, I won't go into all of them here). One of them is music, and my friend John and I had scored seats in the ballot to see German electronica pioneers Kraftwerk, who were playing at the Sydney Opera House as part of the Vivid Festival. They were playing seven shows, performing a different album in its entirety each show, as well as a selection of their best-known songs. We had seats for the "Man-Machine" show on the night of Saturday 25 May.

Thanks to a rookie error of not consulting the footy fixture when booking the flights, I found myself about to board a plane in Sydney at precisely the time the umpire was set to bounce the ball for Hawthorn's Round 9 clash against the Gold Coast Suns in Melbourne. This meant that for the entire duration of the flight, I was going to be out of range and incommunicado, with no way of knowing what was happening.

It's like a kind of unbearable weightlessness, an excruciating limbo, that feeling you have when the Hawks are playing but you have no access to the scores and no way of knowing what's transpiring. The match was happening somewhere and I couldn't experience it, or even conjure it, despite being on an aircraft fitted with a personal iPad (I mean, what's the point of an iPad if all you've got is bland airline entertainment and no way of streaming live AFL?).

I was suffering an existential anxiety, like that feeling you have when you're basking in a new love but you're apart from the object of your devotion, and you try to imagine what they're doing, seeing, even feeling.

But I shouldn't over-dramatise it; after all, we were only playing the Gold Coast Suns. Even though they were on a two-game winning streak, if two in a row can be said to be a streak, those two wins were against weak opposition, whereas with the Hawks, you basically had Mitchell, Hodge, Franklin, Lewis, Sewell, Burgoyne and Roughead against, well, Ablett and a few kids. Even if we were a bit off our game and the Suns were at their peak, surely we'd be five or six goals up by the time I could get the scores.

WTF?

So imagine my disbelief when the captain invited us to turn on our phones and I rustled up the half-time score on the AFL app, only to discover that we were losing. How could we be two goals behind? What on earth had been going on? I got that sick feeling in the stomach, the feeling of impending doom that federal treasurer Wayne Swan must have experienced after spending three years guaranteeing a federal budget surplus only to discover that his calculations were out by, well, $12 billion or so.

On the upside, there was more chance of the Hawks coming back against the Suns than there was of Wayne Swan and the government coming back into contention at the election.

"Just saw the scores ... WTF?" I texted to Chan-Tha, who was at the game.

"I know. We're dropping marks and can't kick straight. Quite sloppy play by us," she replied.

She also texted: "Birchall a late withdrawal" and "Here's a stat – 3 out on the full by Buddy."

I'd read enough. By this stage I'd made my way home from the airport and the third quarter was underway. I noted via the AFL app that we'd hit the front, but the Suns still seemed to be kicking goals with unwelcome regularity.

Surely they couldn't run over us. It would make it very hard to hang it on Collingwood fans if we went and got beaten by the Suns. Mind you, it was still fine to mock Saints fans – getting beaten by the Suns was nowhere near as embarrassing as being beaten by the Bulldogs.

"Sorry, Phillip, not lots of updates, too stressed & frustrated," texted Chan-Tha.

FOOTY FIDELITY

I knew how she felt. It struck me that barracking for a football team is like being in a long-term relationship. Just as with your team, you love your partner to the exclusion of all others, you follow them everywhere and support them through thick and thin, you admire their swagger, you're titillated by their hosiery, their muscle definition, you know their ways and appreciate their potential, you're familiar with all their traits and nuances – yet it is this very familiarity, this deep knowledge and ongoing devotion, that can cause you to grow frustrated when they don't behave as they should, and make you maddened by their antics when they fail to deliver on their promise. You can become annoyed and irritated, but of course you'll never leave them. You'll never renounce them or be unfaithful ...

Okay, so that's where the analogy falls down. Obviously I'll never be unfaithful to Hawthorn, no matter what, but despite being married for 17 years, if Scarlett Johansson sent me a vulgar tweet demanding immediate sexual gratification, I'd be oiling up before you could sing 'We're a happy team at Hawthorn'.

Meanwhile, the Hawks were maintaining a four- to five-goal lead throughout the final quarter. Not great, but really, a win is a win. Melbourne and St Kilda wouldn't be quibbling over the margin if they could get a win, so we should have been thankful that the Hawks had the ability to turn it on and turn it round.

Buddy had shaken off whatever torpor had affected him and slammed on five goals, including a trademark long bomb from 50 metres out on the left-hand flank. Sammy was working the ball forward and was on hand when we needed him most; trailing by 17 points halfway through the third quarter, it was Mitchell who started a forward move with a long handball, and was eventually in the right place to take a handball from Hill and turn onto his left boot to get us going again. Then Burgoyne slotted two over his shoulder and we were back in front. Phew.

BE NICE TO BUDDY

I saw the match highlights online after the event, safe in the knowledge of victory, but I'm glad I didn't have to squirm through it all. Even so, I was shocked to read later that Hawthorn fans had given Buddy bronx cheers after he held a mark. You can't turn on Buddy, people! No matter how many marks he drops or kicks he slices off his boot. Okay, so I wasn't there and didn't see how he was playing in the first half, but presumably he wasn't the only player performing below par. And we shouldn't risk annoying him or giving him a reason to leave. Were all these critics mad! As if he didn't already have enough reasons to leave Melbourne.

He'd had enough abuse during the week. The week wasn't going smoothly for Buddy as it was, and I don't mean the story on the front page of the *Herald-Sun* about him abusing a girl at a nightclub, I mean the shirt he was wearing in the accompanying photo. It looked like something you'd buy at Ishka, a sort of Incan Hawaiian shirt, if that makes sense. It doesn't? Well, you've got the idea. Teamed with a brown brimmed hat – was it a cowboy hat, a leatherette trilby? Either way, you could tell Hawthorn's resident hipster Josh Gibson wasn't with him when he got dressed; he would never have let him walk out the door looking so unstylish. And you also knew it wasn't taken on the night, as there's no way he'd have been let into a Chapel Street bar wearing that.

The girl at the centre of the complaint took to Facebook to publish a litany of unflattering terms to describe Buddy and his behaviour, although mercifully she said nothing about his questionable dress sense.

She also suggested that he was simply a bogan who knew how to kick a ball, an accusation some footy fans, such as the Geelong fan who sat in front of me in Round 1, would find particularly hard to swallow – not that he is a bogan, but that he knows how to kick a ball. Bizarrely, there are those who think Buddy is overrated. These are people who obviously didn't see his Round 3 hurdle goal against Collingwood, his last-quarter tumbling leg-break goal in the 2011 Preliminary Final, his brace of running boundary line goals against Essendon in 2010 or his 100-plus goals in 2008, just to pick a small selection of career highlights. Generally, I find, Hawthorn wins by pretty much the margin that he scores. For example, in this match Buddy kicked 5.2, a total of 32 points, and we won by 26 points. So it's a good thing he was on hand.

Of course, we didn't know what had provoked Buddy to say anything to this girl, let alone anything abusive, since the *Herald-Sun*, that noted organ of truth and justice, didn't provide this perspective.

They had to leave space for the lurid "Exclusive Buddy Boozer" head-line. Are you automatically a "boozer" by virtue of being in a bar? And was it an "exclusive" simply because there was no actual story and no other reputable newspaper – or even *The Australian* – would print it?

This was journalism of the trashiest kind, but the most shock-ing aspect was the byline of Lucie van den Berg ... surely she was no relation of the ex-Hawthorn captain Richie Vandenberg?

Followers of Buddy's Twitter feed did get the odd hint as to what had transpired, and it seemed there might have been another side to the story. As it happened, the story died its own death, not because Buddy apologised, justice prevailed or the truth came out, but because footy, as it so often does, provided a fresh and much juicier scandal to occupy editorial writers and talkback callers.

RACISM ROUND

Buddy's apology to the girl turned out to be of little interest to anyone by the Friday night. It wasn't even the most widely reported apology of the weekend. Or indeed the week that followed.

Indigenous Round of the competition seeks to highlight the tremendous contribution to Australian football of the indigenous community, as well as to celebrate the great indigenous players, past and present. It's one of the AFL's better ideas for a concept round, given that most supporters can look to their own team and applaud a great indigenous player. Or in Hawthorn's case, several, including Buddy, Burgoyne, Cyril and Bradley Hill.

It was a shame, then, that the 2013 Indigenous Round simply highlighted the entrenched and endemic racism in our society. First there was the 13-year-old girl in the crowd who vilified Adam Goodes but who "didn't mean it in a racist way", then there was the footage of the bloke in the crowd ranting about perceived favouritism to Aboriginal players (because white males are so obviously disadvantaged in our society). Then, just as the furore created by these incidents was subsiding, thanks in no small part to some strong ambassadorial work from Collingwood president Eddie McGuire and the dignity of Adam Goodes, Eddie himself suggested on his morning radio show that Adam Goodes could perhaps be persuaded to promote the stage production of *King Kong*.

This sparked a fresh round of explanations, apologies and editorialising. What made Eddie's remarks doubly hard to understand was that they came just five days after he displayed such forthright leadership on this very issue. Not only did he stand up to commend Adam Goodes after Collingwood's match against Sydney, but he showed maturity and added a voice of reason to support and protect the young Collingwood fan at the centre of the storm.

All I could think of to explain the strange disconnect between Eddie's actions on the Friday night and his words on the radio is that on the Friday he was in the role of club president, whereas in the week following he was adopting the persona of a commercial-radio- breakfast-show buffoon. He's obviously a method actor. Not for the first time perhaps, Eddie was finding that he occupied dual roles that were not necessarily compatible.

Eddie, of course, protested that he was no racist, and I believed him, but it hadn't prevented him from making a flippant racist remark on that occasion. It's quite possible to know how you should behave while still doing the complete opposite.

SUNSCREEN WARNING

It may be true that our victory over the Suns could have been more commanding, but then it might be equally true that the Suns are becoming quite accomplished.

This was their third season and many of their younger players had now played 50 games or so, which was about where Buddy, Rough and Lewis were in 2007, their breakout season. Given that, we might need to break out the SPF 30-plus to protect ourselves from the Suns in the coming years, so perhaps we should bask in our victory while we can.

Final scores: Hawthorn 18.10.118 d Gold Coast Suns 14.8.92
Ladder position: 1st
What we learned: Perhaps what Indigenous Round showed us is that it's not quite time to hang the "Mission Accomplished" banner on football reconciliation. Perhaps we need to do more than pat ourselves on the back about our inclusiveness, design special jumpers, acknowledge traditional owners or stage special matches with "Welcome to Country" ceremonies. It might be that these strategies will eventually play a role in bringing about reconciliation, but it seems there's a bit more reconciling to go for a large number of footy fans.
What we already knew: It's pretty easy to say the wrong thing, and if you're on air as much as Eddie, it's almost inevitable that you'll do so at some point. I'm glad my many ill-advised utterances haven't been caught on tape to be held against me for eternity. It's important to remember that footy fans are not defined by their club president. I tend to view most issues through a Hawthorn prism and this is no exception. Eddie's remarks, if nothing else, make some of Jeff Kennett's more outlandish statements as president of Hawthorn sound measured by comparison. As Hawks fans, we often had cause to say to ourselves, "I am not defined by our president," something with which Collingwood fans can now probably identify.

BUDDY MAKES THE WORLD GO ROUND

All Hawthorn matches at this time were viewed through the prism of how Buddy performed. Any return of less than, say, a bag (five goals) and the chattering about his future increased, in equal measure, it seemed, to the hyper-inflationary monetary offers supposedly being dangled before him by Freo, GWS and Carlton. This week we were up to $9 million.

"Greed, for lack of a better word, is good," says Gordon Gekko, as played by Michael Douglas in *Wall Street*. He also says, "What's worth doing is worth doing for money." As I see it, kicking goals for the Hawks is arguably the most worthwhile human endeavour there is, so it is appropriate that Buddy be extremely well remunerated if he is playing for Hawthorn, but if he goes to another club, then his efforts aren't worth a dime.

In this match Buddy kicked two goals, both from free kicks for holding. Of course, had he been awarded a free kick every time he was held in or out of a contest, he might have ended up with 14 goals.

The way James Frawley grappled and groped him looked more like sexual harassment than any legitimate defensive tactics. In fact, had there been a magistrate present, Buddy could perhaps have filed for a restraining order.

This brings us back to Michael Douglas, who was reported in *The Age* during the week as believing that giving oral sex was responsible for him contracting throat cancer. Aside from the medical probabilities of this claim, given that he seemed to have ruled out smoking and drinking as contributing factors, the level of self-congratulation and bragging inherent was also notable. He went on to claim that the cure for this type of cancer – HPV or human papillomavirus – was to administer more oral sex.

I don't know how this works from a medical standpoint – the idea that the cause of the disease can also be the foundation of the cure – but it is eerily similar to the dilemma Hawthorn faced with Buddy at the time: on one hand, he was not having the impact on the game that we knew he could have, yet if he improved and started kicking big bags, then his price would go up and we couldn't afford to keep him, so our only hope was that his output continued to be modest.

Whatever the truth of Douglas's diagnosis, it makes you wonder about the real inspiration behind his wife Catherine Zeta-Jones's films *Death-defying Acts* and *Entrapment*.

HAWTHORN SWEET – MELBOURNE BITTER

"It's a funny game, football" is the sort of expression you might trot out to explain away a surprise result, but there was very little chance this match would provide much in the way of mirth, at least for Melbourne fans.

In fact, ALP strategists would have been more optimistic of victory at the forthcoming federal election than Melbourne's coaching panel ahead of this match. And about as likely to still be in their jobs come September.

It might have been an interesting experiment for the Melbourne coaching panel and the ALP front bench to swap positions for six months and see if either institution fared any worse than was currently the case.

The prospect of a one-sided whitewash didn't appeal to everyone, and that may have explained the poor turnout of only 28,546. It was like playing an interstate team. In fact, only 434 fewer people had turned out the previous week to watch Hawthorn play Gold Coast at the same venue. And this at a venue that has been Melbourne's home ground since 1890.

I did my bit, however. My younger son, Declan, joined us for this match, as did my nephew Max, swelling the numbers by two – not an insignificant number compared to the total. Declan ostensibly barracks for Hawthorn, but also, and quite inexplicably, likes the Demons. I don't know if it is because that's Grandma's team or whether he just likes that they have a mascot synonymous with evil. Probably a bit of both. He also likes Melbourne's Aaron Davey, who was set to make one of his rare injury-free appearances in this match. On this occasion, however, Declan had the good sense to wear his Hawthorn jumper, perhaps having an inkling of the likely result. Max barracks for the Hawks as well, so with Oscar, Chan-Tha and me, we had a good brown and gold contingent to make up for some of Melbourne's shortfall.

Not that I blame Melbourne fans for not turning up – the match pretty much panned out as they would have predicted when they opted instead to catch a matinee of *The Great Gatsby*, pick up a Ralph Lauren polo at David Jones's mid-year clearance or have an afternoon nap rather than go to the game.

In the first quarter, the inside 50 count was 14–8 in Hawthorn's favour. This sounds dominant enough, but what that stat doesn't show is that for some of those 14 entries, the ball stayed inside Hawthorn's forward 50 for five minutes at a stretch, with the Hawks trying to find a way through the morass of Melbourne players cluttering up the backline. In fact, Hawthorn's forward line was more densely populated than some sections of the Great Southern Stand.

The Hawks were applying strong pressure and executing some telling smothers to keep the ball in the forward half. Only poor conversion cost us a match-winning quarter-time lead, scoring 3.9 with five missed set shots, including three from Breust.

There had been much talk of Buddy's form all year, but his value to the side was illustrated by the first goal of the second quarter. Isaac Smith took possession of the ball somewhere near the wing and ran towards goal, with Buddy and three Melbourne defenders running alongside him all the way. With the three Melbourne defenders focused only on Buddy, Smith was allowed to simply keep running and calmly slot the goal.

This was the first of three goals in three minutes to effectively close out the match, with Breust finally nailing a set shot and Burgoyne screwing one through with his left. Then Birchall let fly with a torp that Rough marked on the edge of the goal square.

The Melbourne supporter in front of me had remained stoic and as patient as could be expected throughout all this, but after yet another botched attempt on goal by Melbourne, he finally cracked: "At least get one goal for the match," he bemoaned. His fears were reasonably well founded too. As Melbourne's latest attempt went sailing out on the full, the possibility that the Dees might not score a goal for the entire game had begun to dawn on those who were there. So it came almost as a relief when Jeremy Howe knocked one through off his shin.

They nearly got a second soon afterwards through a series of Hawks mishaps. Gibson took a pass from Smith at half back. Racked by indecision, he feinted left, then right. Then, when the umpire, who was clearly bored with how long it was all taking, called play on, he went left again, but somehow missed his foot in the ball drop and it simply bounced towards David Rodan, the man on the mark. It ended up with Tom McDonald, who bombed it long towards goal, where Brian Lake and Grant Birchall stood waiting beneath it, both courteously leaving it for each other – "After you", "No, after you", "No, look, I insist, after you." During this, it nearly bounced through, except that it fortuitously hit Birchall on the way and so only a rushed behind resulted.

The quarter ended as it began, with a trinity of Hawthorn goals in the space of two minutes. After disappointing conversion in the first quarter, we added 9.1 in the second for a 69-point lead.

An 11-goal lead at half time is enough to win most matches, and that was pretty much the attitude Hawthorn adopted in the third quarter. Melbourne played with more energy and verve in that term and evened up the contest. James Frawley was playing well on Buddy; Chris Dawes was plucking some good marks; and Jack Watts, David Rodan and Nathan Jones kept trying. We were so far in front that I was even able to be magnanimous and cheer along with Declan when Aaron Davey ran in and kicked Melbourne's fifth goal.

That doesn't mean I wasn't a little disappointed that we were outscored by Melbourne in the third quarter. Were we being complacent by subbing Luke Hodge with nearly half a game to go? Whatever key indicators all those stats people in the coaches box were measuring, whatever complex algorithms they were running on their Apple Macs to determine player fitness and fatigue, the fact remains that we were outscored for the quarter. Hence, a good old-school spray from Clarko was required at the break.

Whatever Clarko said seemed to have some effect. From the first bounce of the final quarter, Brad Sewell, who had played an excellent match, took it from the centre and banged it forward, where Sam Grimley took a strong grab and goaled. That was more like it.

Several goals followed, including Breust's fifth, but the real highlights of the final term came from the Poo, who had been energetic all game. In classic Poo mode, he collected the ball in the pocket at Buddy's feet, broke one tackle, barged through another and wheeled around to shoot on goal, only to put it out wide and on the full. Five minutes later he went through the same routine, but this time scored a beautiful goal to cap off an excellent match.

MARK NEELD – IN TOUCH WITH HIS INNER DEMONS

Leading into the match, there had been much speculation in the media about the fate of Melbourne coach Mark Neeld. As if sacking the coach could possibly improve Melbourne in the immediate future, or as if Neeld had arrived to an elite team of ready-made champions, and not a sinking ship that was already half-submerged when he took the wheel. This didn't stop the media stalking him and going through his rubbish bins.

One day I'd like to see all of the AFL coaches camped outside the offices of the *Herald-Sun*, for example, and when Damian Barrett (Damo), Craig Hutchison (Hutchy), Jon Ralph (Ralphy), Mark Robinson (Robbo) or Mike Sheahan (Hey, how come he doesn't have a nickname?) rock up to work the day after a typo has slipped past the subs, bombard them with questions that contravene every basic workplace protection put in place by Fair Work Australia. Questions like "Do you think your job is safe?", "Have you lost the support of the board?", "Will you survive today?", "Have you been asked to resign?" and "Have you thought about stepping down?"

Footage of coaches – or, to give them their full title, "beleaguered coaches" – getting out of cars and walking into a building is not illustrative of anything except the electronic media's utter lack of imagination or sense of a story. When footy journalists apply to their own work the same standards of excellence to which they hold AFL coaches accountable, and when they're happy to forego the safety net provided by strong industrial laws designed to protect them from unlawful sacking, they'll have a lot more credibility when calling for a coach to be sacked.

On the other hand, Melbourne didn't seem to be progressing and they needed to make changes somewhere. The first thing I'd change is the banner they hang around the Northern Stand balcony for Melbourne home matches. Against a backdrop of the Melbourne jumper design, each of their premiership years is listed. There are 12 of them, so it's an impressive enough number, but the problem is that the last year in the sequence is 1964, which is followed by a blank space, presumably awaiting the next premiership year.

When Melbourne won their twelfth premiership in 1964, Hawthorn had just one to their name. In 2014 it will be 50 years since Melbourne won the flag, in which time Hawthorn has nearly caught up.

If I were playing for Melbourne on the MCG and caught a glimpse of that banner as I bounced the ball around the wing, I'd possibly become disheartened and lose control of the ball. Who would want to be reminded of the futility of their task every time they undertake it?

Not all of this was Mark Neeld's fault, of course, but it seemed at the time that his fate was sealed and it was unlikely he'd still be at the helm by the end of the season. In fact, he was probably lucky to have made it to the end of the match.

Final scores: Hawthorn 21.17.143 d Melbourne 6.12.48
Ladder position: 1st
What we learned: More than we really wanted to know about Michael Douglas's mating habits. Also that Melbourne has only 434 more fans than Gold Coast – in Melbourne.

It is perhaps unfair to be critical of an attendance of 28,546 for a match in which the outcome is as close to pre-ordained as you can get in a sporting contest. This counts as a blockbuster by NRL or A-league standards.

What we already knew: After Carlton kicked inaccurately against Brisbane this week, coach Mick Malthouse suggested the full moon was responsible, drawing the ball away from the goals. This comment was largely viewed in a comic light, just another one of Mick's crackpot theories, but before you mock, remember that in Round 7 of 2012, when Hawthorn had last met Melbourne, we kicked 15 goals and 25 behinds, including 3.7 to Buddy. At the time, you'll no doubt recall, the Super Moon, or 'perigee-syzygy' as Scrabble enthusiasts call it, loomed menacingly over us.

The Super Moon describes the period when a full moon coincides with the closest approach of the moon to Earth in its elliptical orbit, making the moon appear bigger in the sky than normal.

It's well known that the moon affects the natural world on Earth – or "impacts the contest", as we might say in footy-speak. The ebb and flow of the tides, or rise and fall of sea levels, changes according to the combined effects of the gravitational forces exerted by the moon and the sun and the rotation of Earth. And this force is stronger when the moon is closer to Earth. Imagine, then, what it was doing to Buddy's natural arc and the flight of the ball – hence Hawthorn's first-quarter inaccuracy, as well as Melbourne's and Carlton's inaccuracy this week.

It was reassuring to think that, as the moon waned and moved further away after this week, its gravitational pull on the Sherrin in flight would lessen and we could expect better accuracy.

SHOULD I STAY OR SHOULD I GO?

BETWEEN THE ROUNDS
3–14 June 2013

Round 11 was the bye round for Hawthorn, and with only six games to preview, and no sex scandals, drug allegations or racism rows to distract us or keep the legion of footy writers engaged in their usual moral hectoring, the media reverted to its default topic for 2013: which team would Buddy play for next year? Not only that, but the "reported" offers rose to $10 million overnight – a degree of hyper-inflation not seen since Germany between the wars.

Former Hawk Campbell Brown, who himself went to the Gold Coast Suns, suggested that Buddy might like to get out of the spotlight in Melbourne. Meanwhile, ex-Richmond legend Royce Hart agreed that yes, Buddy could be useful at Richmond – which, as far as stating the bleeding obvious goes, was a bit like observing that Lionel Messi would fit nicely into Melbourne Heart's starting line-up.

Of course, the footy press gallery showed themselves to be every bit as susceptible to fanciful rumour and flippant suggestion as the Canberra press gallery were when confronted with a whisper of yet another ALP leadership spill, and the journos dutifully proceeded to churn out great tracts of text around every conceivable outcome. How Freo would use Buddy, where Buddy would fit into the Carlton salary cap, what sort of drawcard Buddy would be for

GWS, what sort of compensation Hawthorn would receive for him, whether he could play alongside Tippett at the Swans ...

The only possibility I didn't hear canvassed was of Buddy becoming a code-crosser and playing rugby league or union. But perhaps I just hadn't been paying attention.

Given that there hadn't been one single utterance from Buddy or his management about this issue since the original announcement that he was putting off contract talks until the end of the season, and therefore no material development in the story, you had to admire the ability of our footy media to type themselves into a frenzy over nothing. Imagine if they used all that energy for good?

While I found the whole Buddy saga quite distressing, for my own part I didn't think the AFL was going far enough with free agency. If this was free agency in its purest form, Buddy would be free to play for a different team each week. Perhaps he could be some sort of super-sub, or wildcard selection each week; the team he represented could be determined on a needs basis – which lowly club needed him the most that week, or where he might draw the best crowd. There could be some sort of bidding process, or perhaps Rebecca Judd could pop on that famous red frock and draw a team from a hat in a special ceremony at AFL HQ each Thursday.

IMPORTS VERSUS EXPORTS

All this talk of whether Buddy would stay or go led me to reflect on other great players who have left Hawthorn – and, indeed, on some of the great players who have joined us from other clubs.

Just look at our current backline: Josh Gibson, Brian Lake, Brent Guerra – all imports from other clubs. Then look at Sydney's current midfield, boasting Josh Kennedy and Ben McGlynn – both ex-Hawthorn.

If you lined up those who have joined Hawthorn over the years against those who have left Hawthorn, who would win?

In the spirit of bye week and naming composite representative teams, here are two Hawthorn representative teams: Imports versus Exports.

Players have been selected on the basis of their first club in the VFL/AFL, which is indicated in parentheses.

IMPORTS

Back: Josh Gibson (North Melbourne), Brian Lake (Western Bulldogs), Brent Guerra (St Kilda)

Half Back: Joel Smith (St Kilda), Stephen Gilham (Port Adelaide), Cameron Bruce (Melbourne)

Centre: Stuart Trott (St Kilda), Shaun Burgoyne (Port Adelaide), Russell Greene (St Kilda)

Half Forward: Stuart Dew (Port Adelaide), John Barker (Fitzroy), Darren Kapler (Sydney)

Forward: David Hale (North Melbourne), Jack Gunston (Adelaide), Aaron Lord (Geelong)

Followers: Paul Salmon (Essendon), Norm Goss (South Melbourne), Tony Woods (Collingwood)

Interchange from: Peter Everitt (St Kilda), Anthony Rock (North Melbourne), Lance Picioane (North Melbourne), Luke McCabe (Collingwood), Michael Byrne (Melbourne), Kyle Cheney (Melbourne), Danny Jacobs (Essendon), Shaun Rehn (Adelaide), Matthew Spangher (Sydney), Andrew Demetriou (North Melbourne)

Coach: Allan Jeans (St Kilda)

The Imports team has been largely selected based on their level of performance for Hawthorn rather than for their original club, with the exception of Cameron Bruce, who gets in based on his performances at Melbourne, and because I needed a half-decent half-back flanker and Danny Jacobs just wasn't going to cut it. Likewise, Andrew Demetriou, whose career at Hawthorn was unremarkable but understandably limited due to the fact that, at the time, 1988–89, Hawthorn boasted one of the greatest teams in the history of the game, so getting into it was no easy feat. He is selected on the basis that, as current CEO of the AFL, he's a good man to have on side.

In other points of interest – the current backline takes its place, and it's plain that all our best ruckmen since Don Scott have been imported, with Paul Salmon arguably our greatest import. Well, other than Stuart Dew, that is. Also, it seems over the years that Hawthorn has used St Kilda pretty much as our own development squad.

EXPORTS

Back: Brad Scott (Brisbane), Kelvin Moore (Richmond), Peter Welsh (Richmond)

Half Back: Mark Graham (Richmond), Trent Croad (Fremantle), Campbell Brown (Gold Coast)

Centre: Russell Morris (St Kilda), Terry Wallace (Richmond), Clinton Young (Collingwood)

Half Forward: Darren Jarman (Adelaide), Dermott Brereton (Sydney), Paul Hudson (Western Bulldogs) (Note: 1991 Premiership half-forward line)

Forward: Mark Williams (Essendon), Gary Ablett (Geelong), Daniel Chick (West Coast)

Followers: Greg Dear (Richmond), Barry Rowlings (Richmond), Josh Kennedy (Sydney)

Interchange from: Matthew Robran (Adelaide), Ben Allan (Fremantle), Brent Renouf (Port Adelaide), Luke McPharlin (Fremantle), Ben McGlynn (Sydney), Zac Dawson (St Kilda), Jade Rawlings (North Melbourne), Jonathan Hay (North Melbourne), Steve Malaxos (West Coast), Kevin Heath (Carlton), Ian Scrimshaw (Richmond), Kelvin Matthews (Geelong), Alan Martello (Richmond), Nathan Thompson (North Melbourne), Paul Barnard (Essendon)

Coach: David Parkin (Carlton)

The Exports team has also been selected based on how they played for the Hawks rather than their adopted club, and it's true that many left after their best days had passed: Brereton, Wallace, Martello, Moore, Heath, Hay, Williams. Perhaps this will provide some solace should Buddy leave.

There are a couple of obvious exceptions, such as Gary Ablett Sr, Matthew Robran, Luke McPharlin, Paul Barnard and Josh Kennedy, all of whom you'd have to say did okay after they left the Hawks. But after Robran's tantrum in 1991 after being left out of the Grand Final side for Brereton – I mean, Brereton was the greatest Grand Final player of all time; who would you pick? – I'm pleased that I couldn't find a spot for him in this side either, losing out to, guess who, Brereton again. And if Buddy does leave Hawthorn, you'd squeeze him into the starting line-up as well.

Yet for all of the criticism you might level at Hawthorn for letting Ablett go, as my friend Phillip once observed, we did make seven consecutive Grand Finals immediately after he left, so it's hard to argue that we needed him. Of course, another disadvantage of letting Ablett go is only now becoming apparent, and that is that we missed out on Gary Ablett Jr, under the father/son rule.

Also worth noting is that if St Kilda is our academy, Richmond became pretty much a retirement home for successful Hawks.

Were these two teams, the Imports and the Exports, to compete, I suspect TAB.com.au's Jaimee Rogers would have the Exports as short-priced favourites. While the Imports might have the edge in the ruck, with Salmon, Hale, Everitt and Rehn, on even an average day, you'd back at least one of Brereton, Ablett, Hudson, Jarman, Chick and Williams to fire. Meanwhile, the Imports' forwards of Gunston, Lord, Barker and co. might struggle against the miserly combination of Scott, Moore, Brown and Croad.

Of all the players who have left Hawthorn, the one that upset me most was Kelvin Matthews, who played 99 games before being traded to Geelong in 1978. At the time I had Kelvin's number 4 and his name on my duffle coat. When he left, my mum made me change to Leigh Matthews (3) because it meant that she only had to sew on the first name and a new number. I've still got that duffle coat, and it still has "LEIGH 3 MATTHEWS" emblazoned on its back.

Much as Kelvin was my favourite, he still probably only warrants a spot on the interchange bench. In fact, a team comprising the Exports' extended interchange bench would probably hammer the Imports, plus a few contemporary teams as well. It's a pretty strong line-up if Allan, Barnard and Robran are on the bench. Based on this, you'd have to say that, on balance, Hawthorn has lost more than it has gained over the years. To paraphrase Oscar Wilde: to lose one champion may be regarded as a misfortune; to lose this many looks like carelessness. And if Buddy goes, gross negligence.

RELIGIOUS INTOLERANCE

Footy is often compared to religion, largely because of the unquestioning allegiance to a particular team or creed by its adherents and the fierce devotion of the supporters. There's also the donning of ceremonial vestments, whether it be cassock or duffle coat, the singing of special songs, whether you're belting out a hymn or intoning the team song, and the elevated status of a central figure who is worshipped for their super-human, even celestial powers, such as Christ, Muhammad or Buddy Franklin. Then, of course, there are the sex scandals, but that's another story.

But in addition to all of this, where footy also resembles religion is the enmity that one creed's adherents feel for another's. Just as Protestants and Catholics in Northern Ireland don't mix, and as Jews and Muslims are antagonistic towards each other in the Middle East (well, anywhere, really), so it is with footy fans.

AFL fans will often boast that one of the great things about our game is that fans of opposing sides can sit together at games without rancour or becoming aggressive and combative. And it's true to a large extent. There may not be the rioting and street fighting that you see in a European soccer fixture, or the need to separate fans of opposing teams, but there are ways of showing disdain other than through violence. For example, I harbour a long and enduring loathing of Carlton and consider being a Carlton fan to be a serious character flaw.

As a result, it's no accident that none of my close friends support Carlton. Once I learn someone is a Carlton fan, I know we have nothing in common and that we'll never be close. I show no outward sign of these feelings, except perhaps a barely detectable sour expression, and I make heroic attempts to maintain civility. But I remain as suspicious of Carlton fans as a Shiite might be of a Sunni.

SHOW US YA TATTS!

Of course, it follows that I consider Hawthorn fans to be like-minded sophisticates, sensitive souls who are pure of heart and mind, morally impeccable healers and, above all, good-looking.

So it came as something of a shock when, among those crowding on the post-match Craigieburn train after the Carlton v Hawthorn game, were two Hawk fans, one in his mid-20s, another perhaps in his mid-30s, who spent the entire journey comparing not only their tattoos – which you could argue attests to a certain artistic élan, at least of a gritty urban variety – but also the varying degrees of pain associated with branding the respective body parts.

"What about the behind the ear?" asked elder of younger, referring to the Hawks emblem branded there.

"Nah, not too bad. Tell ya what hurt though. The chest ... Geez, what a killer," he said with relish. Here he lifted his shirt to reveal his stomach emblazoned with large cursive font reading "Blood is thicker than water" (but not as permanent as ink, I thought ... or as nice as champagne).

"That's tough," said the elder admiringly, as if he'd never heard the saying before. Perhaps he hadn't.

"I'll tell ya what hurts the most, though," continued the elder. "The bloody Achilles. Geez, man, that hurt. It's like running a razor blade across your skin." Or a hot branding iron for that matter, I thought.

And on they went with their inventory of tatts, discussing existing tatts, mates with tatts, plans for future tatts and their possible locations, with the elder pausing occasionally to comment again on how much the "bloody Achilles" hurts.

HORSE SENSE

Okay, so not my type necessarily, and perhaps I'm too harsh on Carlton people. After all, former Carlton coach Brett Ratten was doing a great job as an assistant coach at Hawthorn. Just like Carlton, Hawthorn is a broad church and happily accommodates people of all tastes and talents. But even in this there are limits on what is acceptable. On the train on my way to the match I picked up a copy of *MX* and read an article in which Brent Guerra revealed that he has a habit of grabbing the microphone at weddings (presumably the reception) to sing "Horses" by Daryl Braithwaite. This is not an idle occurrence; it's happened 12 times. Not only that, but Dazza is his favourite singer!

This certainly raises questions about Goo's actual age – surely no one under 40 lists Dazza as their favourite singer. But far more disturbing are the questions it raises about his taste in music. Daryl Braithwaite! I imagine Buddy and Gibbo layin' down the grooves with Jay-Z or Kanye in a weights session, or Stratts and Hilly working out to Daft Punk or Flume; Sammy and Hodge would be more your straight rock types, say Springsteen or Coldplay. So it's hard to imagine the reception Goo gets when he tunes the iPod to *Sherbet's Greatest Hits* (is it even available digitally?).

I reflected on this to distract myself from the forthcoming

game against Carlton, about which I held some fears. We were coming off a bye and had played GWS, Gold Coast and Melbourne in the previous three weeks, so I thought the Hawks might be a little bit vulnerable. Added to that, this was to be Chris Judd's 250th game, and if that didn't galvanise Carlton, then surely they must be fired up after their narrow loss to Essendon in the previous round. Plus, they hadn't beaten us since 2006 at the same venue. I recall that occasion as being truly awful, and I was fearful of a repeat.

FALSE DAWN

I arrived late for the match and as I walked in to take my seat, the Hawks were already three goals up. My pre-match fears suddenly seemed stupid and misplaced, baseless anxieties borne of not having seen the Hawks in action for two weeks. Of course we were going to roll them. What was I thinking?

As I took my seat, Breust took a good grab. "Keep it going, Hawkers," I thought. He missed.

And from that moment, 10 minutes into the first quarter, until 10 minutes into the third quarter, when Eddie Betts pushed Ben Stratton into Bryce Gibbs, gathered the ball and ran into goal, Carlton had added 10 goals to our four and it was all looking a little grim.

Along the way we'd turned it over, given away a 50-metre penalty to Matthew Kreuzer for a goal, although it was never clear what the infringement was, fumbled and been out-hustled and harassed by the Blues. One passage early in the third had me feeling anxious. After Jarrad Waite kicked the opening goal of the third to extend Carlton's lead to 17 points, the Hawks were bringing the ball along the wing, where Breust handballed to Hodge, missed him and the ball bobbled over the boundary. It wasn't looking good.

Or sounding good. The match was marred by the two blokes

behind me – one Hawthorn, one Carlton – who yelled "Deliberate!" every time the ball went out of bounds. Every time. If you've ever watched a game of football you'll know how often that is. Hilarious, right? All I could think was that they must have gotten a laugh early on and, desperate for approval, continued to shout it. The only real amusing moment came late in the final quarter after they had eventually grown tired of shouting it, and the umpire finally paid a "deliberate out of bounds" free kick. They missed their big moment.

TRUE FAITH

We needed something and, as usual, it was Sam Mitchell who took it upon himself to turn things around. Charging out from goal, Buddy grabbed the ball and handballed it to Lewis, who got it over to Sammy, who duly slotted one on the left.

After an intervening goal to Eddie Betts, young Taylor Duryea measured a beautiful 40-metre pass to Rough, who marked and goaled. Then came a telling passage in which the Hawks won four one-on-one contests in a row that ended up in a goal to Gunston. This was followed by another attack, culminating in Duryea kicking forward and getting flattened by Waite. The resulting free to Rough put us in front.

The chorus of Carlton booing highlighted either how little football these fans have seen, or that they've become spoilt on a regular diet of cheap free kicks to Chris Judd over the years.

Brian Lake was combining well with Gibbo and Stratton and was playing a great game, taking a series of steadying marks in defence. One of his limitations became apparent early in the final quarter, however: when giving chase to Brock Maclean, who is hardly a speedster, he demonstrated he had the turning circle of the *QEII*, allowing Maclean to put the ball on Dennis Armfield's chest for Carlton to regain the lead.

From there, though, the main men took over. Hodge, of course, put us in front. Then Buddy with a big mark and goal, then Buddy again running on to a pass from Lewis, and finally Hill taking a 40-metre pass from Rough to seal a great come-from-behind win.

BODY LANGUAGE

Of course, all the talk post-match was about Hodge's bump on Marc Murphy, which left the Carlton captain with a broken jaw. To everyone except Carlton coach Mick Malthouse, it was clearly an accidental collision that could just as easily have caused an injury to Hodge. No one wants to see great players get hurt, and that was never more true than on this Friday night, when you could have been forgiven for wishing it was Malthouse, not Murphy, who sustained a broken jaw – if only to stop him going on about it.

The win was made extra-special by Malthouse's tantrum at the end. Being at the game, I didn't see it until I watched a replay the next day, but it was thoroughly enjoyable. When Matthew Richardson, reporting in the Carlton rooms after the match for Channel 7, asked Malthouse how he felt about the game, Mick proceeded to tell him, saying he was "bemused and disappointed. We don't know some of the things that are going on out there."

"What do you mean? What are you bemused at?" asked Richo.

"What do you think I mean, Richo? What would you think I really mean?" snapped back Malthouse. "We lost our captain to a facial break to the head," he added, showing he at least has a firm grasp of basic anatomy.

This was just one incident, apparently, when Carlton didn't receive a free kick. Then he questioned the colour of the Hawthorn doctor's uniform after Carlton players twice kicked the ball in his direction. (Carlton wore navy blue; the doctor wore chocolate brown

– was I missing something? They're a long way apart on the colour wheel. Could it have simply been that the Carlton players in question kicked poorly on those occasions?)

He emphasised that he wasn't taking anything away from Hawthorn, before continuing to do just that and muttering something about just wanting a level playing field – was he reviving the old criticisms about Etihad Stadium's playing surface or was he speaking metaphorically? We'll never know, because he stormed off before Richo could enquire further, not that Richo seemed inclined to do so.

Richo may have looked a tiny bit scared throughout, but he did get a good interview. At least Malthouse doesn't give the usual bland responses, and it showed that he was still passionate about the game and his team. As my friend John observed, however, if you were hitch-hiking to Sydney and Mick Malthouse and Ivan Milat both stopped for you, you'd probably get in with Milat.

Final scores: Hawthorn 15.12.102 d Carlton 13.9.87
Ladder position: 1st
What we learned: If you're going to get a tatt, behind the ear is okay, or on the arm. Even the foot's okay. Just avoid the Achilles – has anyone told Dane Swan?
What we already knew: That the number 23 would make a key contribution at Etihad Stadium this week. Not Buddy this time, although he had played well and kicked four goals, but Mark Bresciano, who wears number 23 for the Socceroos and who opened the scoring for Australia against Jordan in a key World Cup qualifier.
Elsewhere: At Melbourne the CEO was gone, the president resigned and they'd now sacked coach Mark Neeld. This just left a vacuum in footy journalism for more commentary on where Buddy would play next year and what his contract would

be worth. Throwing in a welcome distraction, however, was Jeff Kennett, who put his hand up to be the Dees' president. This brought a mix of mirth and outrage, the main objector being *The Age*'s Caroline Wilson, who was adamant that he should not be president of Melbourne. And I agreed; I thought he should be coach.

ON THE SOLSTICE –
SHORTEST DAY, LONG NIGHT

ROUND 13 – HAWTHORN V WEST COAST
Etihad Stadium, Friday 21 June 2013

The winter solstice is when the sun reaches its furthest north position in the sky before moving back towards the south, marking the turning point in the year's cycle of light – the moment we move from the dormancy, darkness and cold of winter and begin to emerge into the light. In AFL terms, this means we conclude the boring bye rounds and turn for the run home to the finals.

It is the shortest day of the year, and therefore the longest night, which was exactly how it felt to me. I waited anxiously for the siren to end the match as our five-goal lead over the Eagles ebbed away like the midwinter light.

"Solstice" comes from Latin – *sol* meaning "sun" and *sistere* meaning "to stand still" – because it appears as though the sun and moon have stopped moving across the sky ... not unlike our midfield as the final quarter counted down and the Eagles continued to bring the ball forward, where the umpires, like agents of darkness, summoned free kicks for West Coast.

I was at the match with my friend Julian, who, while a Collingwood fan, likes to take in other games as well. Not only did he enjoy the good-quality football in this match, but he was getting tremendous entertainment watching me fret and quibble over every decision that went against us in the dying minutes. The siren finally sounded with the ball in Gunston's hands as he lined up for goal, as sure a symbol as any of the renewal of light and nature's rebirth, of life's triumph over death. And just as the solstice is commemorated with ritual and sacred song, so too this fine victory with a rousing chorus of "We're a happy team at Hawthorn" ringing through the stadium. Although Julian observed that I hadn't seemed particularly "happy" during those final few minutes.

ROUGHEAD – THE SUN GOD

Depictions of Ra, the Egyptian sun god, show a being with the head of a hawk – in some cases complete with wings – so there is no question that we have the sun god, if not other gods, on our side.

And if we had a sun god on the night, it was Jarryd Roughead. Perhaps it was his ginger hair and beard, a fiery mane that meant he at least looked the part. Perhaps it was that Ra might be short for Roughead. Either way, he gave us plenty to worship.

In the first quarter alone he kicked our first two goals, three of the first five and set up our sixth with a deft tap to Breust.

He continued to pluck marks all night and finished with five goals – including a couple just when we needed them. He could have kicked more but was overcome by a deity-like instinct to share, when really the better option might have been for him to hog the limelight. Particularly as his two passes resulted in a grand total of one point.

Our first goal was one of the highlights of the quarter. From the backline Guerra got it to Stratton, who kicked to Hale, who found Hodge, who passed to Breust, who went to Lewis, who got it over the top to Rough running in to an open goal. Seven players, more than a third of the team, combining with seamless fluidity to kick a goal in less time than it took me to type that sentence.

The other highlight of a cracking first quarter in which both teams kicked six goals came courtesy of just one bloke, Eagles ruckman Nic Naitanui. Jumping high, he took the ball directly from a toss in the goal square and was so quick that no one had time to lay a finger on him before he kicked it through.

Naitanui played a great game. In addition to goal of the match, he was the standout ruckman, leaping high to win the tap, and even taking a specky in the final quarter.

THE SUN BREAKS THROUGH

The second quarter, however, was when we established the crucial break that would remain the difference between the teams for rest of the match. Mark Le Cras goaled early to give the Eagles an eight-point lead, though even this was dubious: from my vantage point on level two, you could see the divot he made when sliding to take the mark, and all of it was over the boundary line. Having said that, it was a beautiful kick for goal.

But this injustice was followed by six unanswered Hawthorn goals: Breust, Gunston (twice), Buddy, Rough and Shane Savage. It could have been more had Rough been a tad more selfish and Buddy not been penalised for taking a strong mark while being held – a free kick no one at the ground could quite follow.

The Eagles fought back in the third, but again Rough took a towering mark to kick his fifth and maintain our lead. Buddy tapped cleverly to Breust for another, and Lewis threaded through a nice one from a set shot near the boundary.

In the final quarter the Hawks dominated but couldn't quite score. Nor could Buddy win a free kick, despite being ... well, held isn't the word, more like grappled. It was, I suspect, the winter darkness mounting a final, if futile, resistance before being banished by the post-solstice light, which came from Gunston's post-siren closer.

Final score: Hawthorn 19.9.123 d West Coast 16.7.103
Ladder position: 1st
What we learned: The hyper-inflation surrounding Buddy's "offers" continued to grow at South American rates. The *Herald-Sun* ran a feature during the week reporting that the GWS offer was now up to $12 million over six years. This was just one week after they reported that it was $10 million over the same period and three weeks since they reported it was $9 million. It had gone up by $3 million in just three weeks, a period in which Buddy had kicked just eight goals. Imagine if he was in form! At this rate it would be up to about $30 million over six years by the time he had to make a decision. No wonder he was holding out.

And so far, the journos at the people's paper hadn't presented any evidence of these offers or provided any actuarial tables or fiduciary data to support such figures or why they were escalating so rapidly. No interviews with Buddy, his manager, anyone at GWS or any other club. I wondered if they required a little more of the financial rigour and exactitude of their business reporters. It seemed that every journo who tackled this topic had to add a million per year or it appeared that he or she wasn't doing their job.

I wonder if the GWS accountant was keeping up with these figures. And what sort of salary cap did they have? It seemed nearly as open-ended as the USA's defence budget, or even the Sydney Swans' salary cap.
What we already knew: Watching your team play the Eagles when Perth-born Dennis Cometti is commentating can be a bit like

watching Collingwood with Eddie at the mic. Dennis has been the voice of footy for many years, and his witticisms and puns make most games he calls enjoyable to listen to. I was at the match, but watching it back later I could tell that Dennis really wanted the Eagles to win. He didn't outright barrack like Eddie does, but it was clear where his sympathies lay. Although he went very quiet when the Eagles' Andrew Embley was pile-driving his knees into Ben Stratton's chest.

What we'll never understand: Why Hawthorn was playing a "home" game at Etihad. Must have been to keep the MCG clear for that blockbuster between Melbourne and St Kilda.

Elsewhere: It was hard to fathom what was going on at North Melbourne. After Jack Ziebell was suspended earlier in the year for rough conduct when he bumped Adelaide's Jarryd Lyons, they carped and moaned about the bump being dead – and then this week Brent Harvey was complaining to umpires about being pinched by Fremantle's Ryan Crowley. Pinched! What sort of brute is that Crowley? Compare this to Marc Murphy from the previous week. We hadn't heard a single word of complaint from Marc Murphy over his broken jaw (okay, that might be because he couldn't talk), yet Brent Harvey was carrying on like ... well, Mick Malthouse.

WOMEN'S ROUND ... BOYS' WEEKEND

ROUND 14 – HAWTHORN V BRISBANE
Aurora Stadium, Sunday 30 June 2013

Considering that Indigenous Round served only to expose the blatant racism still endemic in our society, it was only fitting that we should commence Women's Round by deposing Australia's first female prime minister.

And even though Julia Gillard is a Bulldogs fan (talk about setting yourself up for failure), it's still a step up from being a rugby fan. Say what you like about Julia Gillard – an invitation a number of people were all too happy to take up, as it happened – but at least for a few years we had a PM with an understanding of what's really important in life – football! The last prime minister before her to understand anything about football was Malcolm Fraser in the '70s, and he was Carlton, so it was hard to take any pleasure in that.

The fact that the Dogs went down to the Demons on Saturday night must have capped off the week perfectly for Gillard. You wonder what was the more soul-destroying and humiliating loss for her – the prime ministership to Rudd or the football to the Demons.

A PRIDE OF LIONS – THE BOYS' WEEKEND

The Hawks were up against the Brisbane Lions in Launceston for Women's Round, but unfortunately I wasn't going to be on hand to catch the game. Once a year I join a group of friends for a boys' weekend where we travel interstate to a game that doesn't involve any of our teams (Hawthorn, Richmond, Sydney, Collingwood and Geelong). As you can tell, this rules out a number of options. Plus, I refuse to watch Essendon and Carlton, so that limits it even further.

This annual rite began in 2009, when we travelled to Launceston to see the Hawks play Brisbane. Hawthorn lost that day; hence the rule about going to games that don't involve our teams. The idea is that if none of our teams are playing, no one has to feel anxious about the match and sulk afterwards. Of course, for me the catch is that I feel doubly anxious because I can't watch Hawthorn. And as with our earlier match against the Suns, I was on a plane for the majority of the match so didn't have access to score updates.

Even so, I was quite confident the Hawks would defeat Brisbane, despite the Lions' amazing win over Geelong the week previous. The Lions kicked a goal after the siren to win the match. Ashley McGrath, playing his 200th game, marked on the siren and went back and slotted the ball from 50 metres to defeat the Cats. This was after Geelong had held a 53-point lead. What Hawks fan didn't smirk as the ball sailed through and Lions players piled on top of one another in celebration, while the Cats looked about in disbelief before trudging off?

Who didn't scan the background in the hope of catching a glimpse of Geelong's Tom Hawkins, to delight, just a little bit, in his disappointment? It might be churlish, but after he'd kicked a fairly similar post-siren goal to sink the Hawks in 2012, we could take some small measure of satisfaction in watching the same thing happen to Geelong.

Back to our boys' weekend, and the Lions, as it turned out, had another post-siren kick that, if successful, would have seen them snatch victory. Another long kick on which rode the fortunes of the match and the hopes of thousands of visiting fans who had traversed oceans to be there. That time, however, the ball fell short and the Wallabies took it out of play to secure victory.

Of course, I'm referring here to the rugby-playing British and Irish Lions, not the native AFL Brisbane breed, who were never going to get close to the Hawks. For a start, they had to travel all the way from Queensland to Launceston, which is a journey not only over distance, but through biospheres and ecosystems. Like Fremantle travelling from Perth, it was going to take them a quarter to achieve a functioning body temperature, by which time we'd have established a match-winning lead.

HOW DO YOU LIKE THEM APPS?

We'd enjoyed a good weekend on the Gold Coast, where we saw the Gold Coast Suns play Adelaide at Metricon Stadium, sat in an Irish pub to watch the Wallabies play the British and Irish Lions and Geelong play Fremantle, and caught a bit of Wimbledon and the opening night of the Tour de France. Plus, as the curtain-raiser to the Suns v Crows match, we saw Coorparoo v Zillmere in the Queensland Women's Under-18 AFL competition as part of Women's Round.

All of these events were good in their own way, but none was as satisfying as watching the Hawks. It's ersatz sport, a poor simulacrum, like watching a tribute band (The Australian Doors Show rather than The Doors) or voting for the ALP – you can do it, but there's no emotional investment and no payoff, and in the case of the latter, you come out of it feeling just a little bit grubby.

So I sat through my two-hour flight as impatiently as any voyeur seated in the stalls at Her Majesty's Theatre waiting for Jerry Hall to disrobe in *The Graduate*. When I was finally able to flick on the AFL app, I saw that we held a reasonably comfortable 44 to 21 lead two-thirds of the way through the second quarter.

But five minutes later the score still stood at 44–21, and no amount of prodding at my phone's screen could move it along. And throughout the ride on the courtesy bus back to the car, the score still stood at 44–21. What was going on down there? Or more precisely, not going on. According to the app, it wasn't half time, yet neither team was scoring. Was there a ground invasion? Had enraged Hawthorn fans taken Buddy hostage and held up the game until he signed a new contract? Or was it just that the AFL app wasn't working? It was a desperate and frustrating situation, worse than Jerry Hall's zip getting stuck on the way down.

A SCROLL OF GOALS

My phone sounds a series of percussive pips when a text message comes through. It had been on for approximately 15 minutes since I'd landed when it suddenly erupted in a drum solo of beats as Chan-Tha's texts piped through in a manic burst like a batch of popcorn. It was like the birth of techno in my pocket.

And there, at last, was the updated story laid out in a happy scroll of goals:

Lewis got our first from a free kick for in the back.
Buddy got a behind ... standard Buddy.
But we love him.
Just messed up a certain goal.
Gunston goal. Hawks 15–7.
25–8. Can't believe we're not thrashing them.
38–8. Go Hawks..
44–14 – seem a bit flat. Why are we letting them score?
Great goal by Buddy outside 50.
Even better one by Buddy a minute later!!
57–35 half time.

Okay, so that was an advance on the app score, but my calculation of game time suggested there was still a lag between text time and the actual time. Another staccato burst from my phone and the follow-up texts came through:

Ellis subbed out for Simpkin.
Gibbo fell on his head – might never recover …
It's ok – his face will be unscarred …
Shiels injured – might require amputation …
Uh-oh …
Lions coming back!

I sensed the panic in her texting thumb.

By this stage I'd picked up the car, and the commentators on the radio were talking in reassuring tones about Hawthorn turning it on in a quick burst. Judging by the relaxed chatting of the commentary team, it was evidently three-quarter time and whatever had caused Chan-Tha's alarm had clearly passed.

When they eventually gave the score of 15.15 to 7.7, I was able to relax, with only a momentary thought that the Lions had come back from a similar position the previous week to defeat Geelong. Surely not again.

And so it proved. I listened to the final quarter on the radio as Chan-Tha's satisfied texts continued to pipe through, providing a more succinct description of the events unfolding at Aurora:

Savage goal.
Buddy lining up for goal.
Got it!
Savage 3 goals!

Another happy win – our twelfth in succession, to equal a club record from 1961. And only arch-nemesis Geelong standing in the way of setting a new record next week. No problem, then.

The good news to come out of the match was that Josh Gibson was okay. His heavy fall looked horrific, but happily there were no scars ... his looks remained intact. With Buddy potentially leaving, we needed Gibbo more than ever, not just for repelling opposition attacks from the backline but to model our Hawk couture in the Hawks Nest catalogue next season.

Final scores: Hawthorn 21.17.143 d Brisbane 12.13.85

Ladder position: 1st

What we learned: That the AFL hasn't learned. The lesson of Football Park in Adelaide and VFL Park in Melbourne is that stadiums need to be built near public transport. If you want people to be able to get to them, that is. Metricon Stadium on the Gold Coast is a great venue, but it's in the middle of nowhere and is virtually impossible to get to.

What we already knew: In an interview on Fox Footy's *On the Couch* earlier in the week, Essendon captain Jobe Watson admitted to being injected with a substance which he was later told may have contained banned performance-enhancing drug AOD-9604. The drug is banned by the World Anti-Doping Agency (WADA), but Jobe said he thought it was legal at the time. Well, that's good enough for me! What concerned some observers, however, is that Watson was permitted to play the following Friday. Most vocal in this regard was the West Coast Eagles home crowd, which hooted him every time he gathered the ball, but it was unclear whether they were expressing a moral view on the issue, or were just annoyed that he was instrumental in Essendon securing an important victory over the Eagles.

My favourite summation of the incident came from *Herald-Sun* journo Mark "Robbo" Robinson, who wrote that Jobe Watson isn't a drug cheat, but could be found guilty of this offence. Could be? Didn't he admit to it? Now, I don't pretend to be an expert in the legal nuances surrounding this issue, but you could argue that the very definition of a drug cheat is someone who has been found guilty of drug cheating. Or to put it more simply, Robbo, "ipso facto".

The consensus among football reporters was that Jobe shouldn't be stripped of his Brownlow medal because he is a "top bloke". And from what I've seen and heard from Jobe in the media, this is true, he is. Were he not a "top bloke", of course, it would presumably be different. This "top-blokeness" bit must come under a sub-clause in ASADA's anti-doping code. One wonders what Ben Cousins makes of it all: banned for a year for bringing the game into disrepute, largely because he could go on a bender and still pick up 40-plus possessions. There's as much to admire in that as condemn.

The day after: Florine Marchand, Peter Delaney, Chan-Tha Birch, Phillip Taylor and Oscar Taylor.

David and Liz Moore with their newborn son, Oliver, in a pretty cool baby bath. Oliver was born two days before the match.

Chris, David and Frank Thompson with Sonja Bedford at the MCG after the
Grand Final.

Happy kids at Hawthorn: Cheyenne (left) and Tyrone (right).

Romayne Perera, a happy Hawk!

The Stone family celebrates the Preliminary Final win over Geelong: brothers Justin, Josh, Eugene and Alexander Stone, and Justin's son Charlie.

Chris Thompson's two dachshunds, Rudi and Gretel, on their pre-match
Grand Final Day lucky walk. Rudi is more commonly known on Brunswick
Street as "Buddy Frankfurt".

Michelle Sherriff, Fiona Youlten and Kath Youlten at the game.

Linda Williamson's photo of a car-park picnic before the match.

Ned Penfold – Hawthorn's lucky charm. The Hawks have made it to the Grand Final every year since he was born!

Young fan Bart Sovereign
supporting his Hawks.

Mikayka and Nikita
Thompson at the MCG.

Gay O'Keefe, Cheryl Robinson
and Ryan O'Keefe after the siren at
the Grand Final.

Brad Hopkins, Ollie Howe and Brett Attrill about to head onto the MCG to hoist Hawthorn's 2013 Grand Final banner. Nothing says success like sequins!

Jennie Rogers and Emma Rogers celebrating on the MCG as the Grand Final After Party winds down.

Lauren Porter amongst the cheer squad at the 2013 Grand Final – "the happiest day of my life!"

Madeleine Sheppard and Tiana Reid showing their excitement in the Hawthorn cheer squad after the 2013 Grand Final win.

Stephen and Lauren Solomonson took in the match from Minnesota, USA.

A special celebration: Mrs Jean Daniels (centre) passed away in November 2013 after a long fight with cancer, but not before she'd seen one more Hawks premiership. Left to right: Charli Rose McConnell, Chace Daniels, Matthew Daniels, Jean Daniels, Jamaal Lewis, Jasmine Daniels, Lucie McConnell, Jett Daniels. On the floor: Isaiah Daniels, Jan Daniels and Ella Daniels.

Herald Sun
Herald Sun WE'RE FOR THE GREATEST GAME
Herald Sun WE'RE FOR THE FANS
VICTORIA
Herald Sun

Celebrating the win – from left to right: Kate Mallett,
Bruce Ludeman, Felicity Ludeman, Ian Senior

Donna May shows off her new ink.

KENNETT'S OTHER CURSE

Much had been made of Jeff Kennett's pronouncement on the eve of the 2009 season that Geelong didn't have the mental toughness to defeat Hawthorn in big games. Predictably, we hadn't beaten them in any of our 10 meetings since, finding any number of ways to lose in the last minute, including twice with the very last kick, in what had become known as " the Kennett curse".

Of course, the more oxygen breathed into the notion of the Kennett curse, the more potency we granted to Jeff's pronouncements, and the more he'd feel vindicated to keep making them. Reason enough then to defeat Geelong at last and end the "curse".

Less discussed, however, was Kennett's other curse. After winning the 2008 premiership, Jeff, in exuberant celebratory mode, and possibly under the influence of a particularly ripe herbal tea, announced that Hawthorn would never trade any players from the 2008 premiership side.

Since then, though, the players who represented Hawthorn that day have been slowly disappearing, one by one off the list. Like opponents of Pinochet in Chile, they were gradually going missing. Of the 22 players selected to represent Hawthorn on that glorious day, 11 of them, exactly half, were no longer with the club – either traded, debilitated or delisted. And of those who were traded to other clubs, none had performed at a level anything like their premiership heroics. Many of them had been afflicted by career-interrupting injury or loss of form.

It was time to ask, what had happened to them?

Shane Crawford – retired
Stephen Gilham – traded to Greater Western Sydney
Trent Croad – retired through injury
Mark Williams – traded to Essendon, where he never recaptured his Hawthorn form
Brent Renouf – traded to Port Adelaide (oh, the inhumanity!), rarely played
Campbell Brown – traded to Gold Coast Suns, had been suspended for nearly as many games as he'd played
Stuart Dew – retired
Chance Bateman – retired through injury
Robert Campbell – retired through injury
Rick Ladson – retired
Clinton Young – left for Collingwood under free agency; had been injured ever since

If you included the players named as emergencies for that Grand Final – Tom Murphy (delisted), Simon Taylor (delisted) and Travis Tuck (delisted) – then 14 of 25 were no longer with us.

Despite Kennett's grand familial gesture, the team that won on that famous day had been gradually dismantled until it bore very little resemblance to the 2013 side. In fact, only seven members of that premiership team would be out there in our Round 15 match against Geelong.

So, while everyone was focused on the Kennett curse as it related to match results, were we perhaps overlooking an equally sinister Kennett pronouncement that had seen fit, young men with bright futures drop one by one, some succumbing to mysterious career-ending injuries, others to irreversible form slumps, one to GWS and in one particularly tragic case, a player becoming so brain-addled he elected to go to Collingwood, where he had since been incapacitated?

Was this the other Kennett curse? A curse so virulent it struck down men in their prime and cast them off, taking them from the comfort of Hawthorn's bosom and forsaking them in the wilderness. A curse that robbed them of their futures and condemned them to the badlands of retirement or worse, Port Adelaide.

We needed to find a way to reverse these curses and end the evil influence of their instigator. And quickly, because among the players left were Franklin, Hodge, Mitchell, Roughead, Lewis, Rioli and Sewell. We needed an antidote before the curse struck them.

On a side note, Geelong had nine players from the side that lost in 2008 playing in the Round 15 clash, 10 if you count Josh Hunt, who was an emergency. Of Hawthorn's line-up, nine players had never played in a Hawthorn side that had defeated Geelong, though admittedly one of them was ex-Cat, Jonathan Simpkin.

So Hawks fans headed into the match against Geelong with the sense of weary dread and resignation to which recent history had conditioned us. With 12 consecutive wins and top position on the ladder, however, we could still entertain a flicker of hope that this would be the night.

#GROUNDHOGDAY11 #NOTAGAIN #EVENABRITCANWINWIMBLEDON WHILEWESTILLCANTBEATGEELONG

My God, it had come to this – a British tennis player had won Wimbledon and the Hawks still couldn't beat Geelong. The fact that Andy Murray was actually Scottish was of very little consolation. At this rate the Socceroos would win the World Cup before we ever beat the Cats.

I wondered how Robbo from the *Herald-Sun* would see it. The great scribe who wrote of Jobe Watson that he wasn't a drug cheat but could be found guilty of drug cheating might furrow his brow in philosophical contemplation, unsheath his quill and inscribe on his parchment with great flourish something along the lines of: "Hawthorn can beat Geelong, but they'll go down in history as not having beaten them."

MATHEMATICALLY POSSIBLE

It was Round 15, that time of year when teams sitting two or even three games outside the eight, like Carlton and Adelaide, started to talk in terms of it being mathematically possible for them to make the finals. At Hawthorn we thought that way about Geelong: it was mathematically possible to beat them, we just couldn't beat them. We'd examined it from every perspective and saw that we could beat them in just about every way – theoretically, geographically, historically, economically, scientifically, ethically, romantically – just not actually.

But it was mathematically possible. In 2011 we finished third; in 2012 we finished second, so you can see the numerical sequence taking shape here: in 2013 we'd finish first. To do this we had to beat Geelong at some point, so in this sense at least, it was mathematically possible.

HISTORICALLY POSSIBLE

As we trudged from the G to Flinders Street after the match, my son Oscar asked if we'd ever been to a match and seen Hawthorn defeat Geelong. A couple of people nearby chuckled at such wide-eyed innocence.

"Of course!" I scoffed, then had to hurriedly try and think if, indeed, we had revelled in such an occasion (he hadn't been able to join me at the 2008 Grand Final, as members of the MCC can't take guests to the Grand Final). "Once upon a time ..." I began and I launched into the tale about the only time we'd sat together to watch Hawthorn triumph over the Cats. It was Round 22, 2006, the final match of the home-and-away season, and neither team had any chance to make the finals, Geelong having blown their chance the previous week. Oscar and I sat in a forward pocket at Etihad Stadium and cheered on a resurgent Hawthorn as they rolled the Cats by 61 points, with Buddy kicking a stunning goal in one of his early outings for us.

On our quiet journey home by train, I reflected on other great Hawthorn triumphs over Geelong ... not including the great 1989 and 2008 Grand Finals, that is.

Round 4, 2007: Just before Geelong's famed run of wins in 2007
that resulted in a drought-breaking premiership, we knocked

them off by four points at Kardinia Park. They've never invited us back.

Round 7, 2002: We hold Gary Ablett Jr to just seven disposals – admittedly, it's only his third game – and the Hawks turn in one of their best performances of the year to win by 52 points at the G.

Round 6, 1999: Undermanned and out of form, the Hawks again defeat the more fancied Cats at Kardinia Park when Daniel Harford snaps the winning goal just minutes from the end.

Second Semi Final, 1991: The Hawks dominate the first quarter but kick 3.11 to 2.1. Geelong takes over in the second half, with Gary Ablett Sr starring, until Darren Jarman slots the winner from the boundary line. Tragically, Morrissey (the English singer, that is, not number 35 for the Hawks) cancels his show scheduled for later that night at Festival Hall.

Round 6, 1989: The Hawks trail by 49 points at half time, but, inspired by Dermott Brereton, Gary Ayres, Gary Buckenara, John Platten and Jason Dunstall, storm home to win by eight points in one of the greatest games of all time. The only game that comes close for the year is the Grand Final between the same teams, which of course Hawthorn won by six points.

Round 22, 1987: The final round of the season. Geelong needs to win to make the finals and they lead all day, until the final minute, when Dunstall takes two marks, kicks two goals and the Hawks prevail by three points to knock them out of the finals. Over at the Western Oval in Footscray, Melbourne fans glued to transistors erupt when Hawthorn wins, as this puts them into the finals for the first time since the mid-'60s.

Round 21, 1986: The Hawks lead by three points at half time in an even contest, then kick 25 goals to three in the second half (12 in the third quarter and 13 in the fourth) to win by 135 points, with Dunstall kicking nine. You really had to be there.

Round 12, 1985: The notorious Matthews/Bruns match – Mark Jackson takes it in turns to beat up the Hawthorn backline, then Leigh Matthews hits Neville Bruns and is the first VFL player charged by the police for an on-field action. Hawks by 29 points!

Round 21, 1978: John Hendrie bounces one through from 40 to put the Hawks in front by two points, and Gary "I Touched It!" Malarkey earns his nickname. Hawthorn cheer squad leader Spiro gets hauled away by the police for throwing cut-up paper in celebration of the winning goal, and is marched around the boundary line.

So it is at least historically possible for us to beat Geelong, and even if we don't achieve that again in my lifetime, perhaps one of my sons or one of their sons will live long enough to see it happen.

SAME OLD SAME OLD

It was a cold, miserable and wet night in Melbourne so we ascended to level four, where we could sit undercover. Oscar's friend Jack was with us, a Cats fan, and as we took our seats, we greeted my friend Martin and his family, also of a Geelong persuasion, who were arriving at the same time. After the Grand Final in 2008 Martin was the first person to find me and shake my hand in congratulations. Of course, he's also the first one through with a mocking text when the Cats defeat Hawthorn, so I had to steel myself and try to be calm and gracious no matter what the result.

"The Cats will win," his six-year-old son, Xavier, said to Oscar before the game started.

It appeared that the match was over fairly early, with the Cats taking the early advantage and kicking away to a good lead. The good thing about this was that we didn't have to sit there grinding our teeth and waiting to be overrun. And although we held them for the next two quarters, we were finding it difficult to score ourselves.

For some time it had appeared that our inability to beat Geelong was a pathological condition, that it was actually Hawthorn that defeated itself, and not necessarily the result of anything Geelong was doing. An inventory of our misses from set shots in this match backed up this hypothesis: Hale, Roughead, Hodge, Franklin, Breust. Now, I love Breeuuust, but why can't he just kick a set-shot goal against Geelong? Just for me. From quarter time, however, Geelong was missing shots as well.

The third quarter was particularly mistake-ridden, with both sides missing targets, fumbling and shanking kicks. The teams kicked just 1.10 between them. There may well have been enormous pressure out there and perhaps the conditions were difficult – though it was difficult to tell from the comfy position I'd taken up in the Hugh Trumble Bar in the MCC Members' – but you couldn't help thinking that if these were the two best sides, then what were the remaining 16 like? Cyril's return after missing eight matches due to the hamstring injury he sustained in Round 5 was really the only highlight of the quarter.

Despite being well out of it all night (4.11 at three-quarter time!) the Hawks mounted their usual late flurry and slotted five goals in nine minutes to get us excited and out of our seats. The fourth goal came courtesy of an interchange free kick to Hale and got us within a few points. There were reports the interchange free kick was actually a mistake, but I don't think so. It may not have been technically correct, but I suspect the umpires paid it as part of some larger, perverse agenda of wanting to see us come agonisingly close yet again.

Either way, after sitting in glum silence for most of the match, we were suddenly up and chanting as an unpromising situation looked like it was turning.

Sadly, that was where the excitement ended. The main talking point of the final quarter was when Joel Corey knocked himself out. Geelong fans at the ground seemed to find Sam Mitchell at fault, even though it was Corey who tackled Mitchell from behind and pulled him backwards, from where gravity took over and brought Mitchell crashing down on top of him. But of course if Geelong fans were able to discern between right and wrong, they wouldn't be Geelong fans in the first place.

The incident halted the match while the medical staff attended to Corey, and the Hawks' momentum dissipated. As is the way with these games, Geelong settled and held on to win another close one, leaving Oscar and me to be taunted by Martin's six-year-old son.

"I told you we'd win," he boasted. This is someone who has never known Geelong to lose to Hawthorn, which makes it tough to tease him about the 1989 or 2008 Grand Final results.

SWEET SUBMISSION

All of the media blather about the Kennett curse and the Cats pact simply served to mask what might have been the real reason behind this protracted sequence of narrow losses to Geelong, which now stretched to 11 – we love it! Perhaps the Hawks get off on it in some perverse way. It could be that the closer the loss, the more erotically charged we become.

Human sexuality is a mysterious phenomenon, unique and diverse. Some men like Asian chicks in Hawthorn gear, while others like Scandinavian chicks in Hawthorn gear; who can fathom such binaries?

Who can really explain their own preferences, let alone someone else's? One man's predilection is another man's peccadillo, as they say; some crave a caress while others take their pleasure through pain.

And just as some people like to crawl around the floor wearing an adult nappy with a studded leather bridle in their mouth, perhaps Hawthorn gets off by taking it roughly from Geelong and narrowly losing matches we could have won.

In BDSM (bondage and discipline, dominance and submission, sadism and masochism) lore, there are three roles, the master or mistress (top), the submissive or sub (bottom), and the switch, someone who likes to swing between the roles of dominance and subservience.

Hawthorn takes the submissive or bottom role in these BDSM sessions – submitting to Mistress Geelong and taking our orders from her. She exerts her feline wiles and extends her sharp claws to demonstrate her expertise in the dark erotic arts of punishment, discipline and humiliation. Just how we must like it. Being under their control and experiencing pleasure through the discomfort, pain and suffering inflicted on us.

Anyone familiar with the type of BDSM practices enacted in any dungeon worthy of the name will recognise much of what took place between Hawthorn and Geelong on that Saturday night of Round 15. Buddy was engaging in wrestling most of the night, I think Joel Corey was trying to tie up Mitchell in some sort of human bondage act (he just didn't utter his "safe word" in time), our forward line was enjoying being "smothered" and who knows what was going on in some of those packs.

Scan the menu of services available at The Correction Centre and you'll see that guests have a choice not only of golden showers, but also of brown showers. Now, it doesn't take a particularly perverse imagination or diverse dalliance to understand what this means – and we'd been taking the football equivalent for five years. The only possible explanation I could come up with was that we must have loved it – couldn't get enough of it, in fact – otherwise why did we keep doing it? It was about time we "switched".

Final scores: Geelong 11.16.82 d Hawthorn 10.12.72
Ladder position: 1st
What we learned: The torrent of Twitter abuse levelled at the winner of the Wimbledon women's title, Marion Bartoli, for being arguably less attractive than her opponent, Sabine Lisicki – or "not a looker", in the words of BBC commentator John Inverdale – told us that sports fans are shallow and fixated on some absurd notion of a "beautiful ideal", and that sports fans on Twitter are even worse than sportspeople on Twitter; #whatisitwithyoupeople? On the other hand, it is perhaps recognition of what constitutes the beautiful ideal that explains Hawthorn's strong membership and big crowds.
What we already knew: Hawthorn and Geelong were surely now the premier fixture in the AFL season, a point voted on by the football public this Round 15 weekend, with 85,197 people turning up to watch, compared to the measly 78,224 who turned up to watch the previous night's clash between "traditional rivals" Carlton and Collingwood.

Sam Mitchell is a superstar and was truly great in this game against Geelong. Our best chance of winning big games comes when he has the ball. If GWS knew anything about football, they'd have been chasing him instead of Buddy.

WINTER MASTERPIECES – HAWTHORNISM

The NGV's Winter Masterpieces exhibition, *Monet's Garden*, showcased some of the major works by the great French impressionist Claude Monet, with particular emphasis on his paintings of the waterlilies that he cultivated and which flourished on his property in Giverny.

Impressionism was a nineteenth-century art movement that originated in Paris, with Monet as one of its earliest and most celebrated practitioners. It is characterised by pictures that focus not so much on formal lines, detail and realism, but on an overall visual effect that captures changes in light and movement. The artists used short brush strokes and intense colours to convey a sense of bristling energy. Colours bleed into one another, creating a blur or shimmer of movement.

Not unlike watching Hawthorn play Port Adelaide *en plein air*, really, with brown and gold stripes mixing with teal, white and black over a verdant green field and the crowd dotting the background: Hawthorn's short kicks mirroring the short brush strokes, the quick ball movement, morphing bodies and polychromatic palette all combining to create a convergence of vivid colours and effervescent, vibrant action. And that was just the first five goals that came in an audacious brown and gold blur from Rough, Gunston, Savage, Lewis and Gunston again.

To complete the illusion, it had been raining heavily in Adelaide during the week and the surface of AAMI Stadium was nearly as damp underfoot as Monet's famous pond.

A DRINK AT THE LINC

The match was being played the day after my visit to the Monet exhibition, and I was at my local, The Linc in Essendon, to watch it.

Port's recent resurgence after beating both Sydney and Collingwood, our flaky record at AAMI Stadium, Ken Hinkley in the box for Port (the architect of many Geelong victories over Hawthorn in recent years), and no Sewell (dropped) or Buddy (injured) gave cause for unease going into this match. Even watching in a pub, I felt as nervous and jittery as an Australian middle-order batsman about to face Jimmy Anderson or Graeme Swann.

The first quarter may have dispelled these nerves somewhat, with Hawthorn playing slick, clean footy to lead by 22 points at quarter time. This second quarter served to reinforce my pre-match disquiet, however, as Port upped the tempo. Playing a quick, attacking game, Port moved the ball swiftly, spread well and created multiple scoring opportunities through Robbie Gray and Brad Ebert. Even Angus Monfries was getting the ball. When Jay Schulz kicked truly, Port was within four points. And then Cyril hobbled off with a possible injury. Time for another pot.

Happily, Gunston snapped a nice – dare one say "Buddyesque"? – goal on his left to restore our advantage, followed by another to Savage to give us a slightly more comfortable lead of 12 points at half time.

The Linc is a weird pub, and on this day the bar staff were not as attentive to thirsty patrons as they could be. It being a fairly miserable afternoon outside, the lounge was gradually filling and little knots of people stood at the bar for minutes on end with no one being served.

It's not like the staff were uncaring Gen Ys who were busy texting, taking selfies or trying to advance to the next level of Candy Crush; they were simply not around or were tending to some unseen crisis in the gaming area. Perhaps they were just trying to recreate the genuine footy experience of making people wait five minutes to get a drink. And given that a bowl of chips costs $8, it was almost like being at the game. One thing was for sure, you certainly couldn't accuse them of ignoring their obligations with respect to the responsible service of alcohol.

"NOTHING UNTOWARD THERE"

I eventually secured a fresh pot and sat down to take in the third quarter. And it began with a bang, at least for Port's Tom Logan, who was flattened by Burgoyne – a play that led to the opening goal of the quarter through a series of slick handballs until Isaac Smith slammed it through.

It was difficult to tell if Burgoyne's bump on Logan upset Port fans because they'd been booing him from the opening bounce for having the temerity to leave them – even though it was getting on for four years since he'd left. The Snowtown killers would have received a better reception. Reports during the week from the Tour de France that spectators had sprayed urine on English rider Mark Cavendish to express their unhappiness over his part in a pile-up during the race for the line made me fear for what might befall Burgoyne before the end of the match. Luckily, he was already wearing brown and yellow.

While no free kick was awarded at the time, Burgoyne ended up taking a two-match ban for the incident. Tom Harley's commentary after viewing the incident in replay was: "Nothing untoward there; just good, solid contact from Burgoyne."

If nothing else, the aggression intensified after this, with Mitchell going down behind play. Ben Stratton also went down, but this was through his own doing more than anything else. The Poo put it out in front of him in space. Stratton gathered and ran towards an open goal, but his bounce went askew and as he bent to retrieve it he ducked into the knee of Chad Wingard, who had by then caught up to him. Stratton collapsed on top of the ball, making no attempt to dispose of it. Well, yes, he was unconscious, but even so ... Amazingly, however, the umpire paid Stratton the free kick. For a push in the back!

If Wingard touched his back, it was only after Stratton had been lying on the ball for several seconds. As Stratton was too groggy to take his kick, Rough obligingly stepped in and duly slotted his third to give us a 24-point lead. You can imagine how graciously the Port fans took that.

HAMISH'S HOMEWORK

The most revealing part of the third quarter came soon after when Angus Monfries took possession on the forward line, panicked and handballed to Travis Boak, who had Duryea right behind him. Our boy Duryea immediately brought Boak to ground with a solid tackle and earned a free kick.

Angus Monfries's quick handball put Boak in an awkward position, but I was amused by Hamish McLachlan's commentary on Channel 7. Trying to find an apt analogy to elucidate the action for viewers, Hamish delved into his considerable life experience, scanned his store of literary antecedents, turned over a few phrases in his mind to get a sense of their heft and tone, let his inner raconteur off the leash and expounded: "He was put under pressure. He was asked to write a really hard essay."

"Write a really hard essay!" This seemed an unusual choice of analogy for football commentary, even considering that many contemporary players study part-time. Hamish was perhaps referring to his own academic endeavours, but in doing so inadvertently illustrated that his grasp of metaphor was as unsure as that of a player trying to gather the Sherrin cleanly on the slippery surface.

Duryea's tackle must have inspired the team because the remainder of the quarter saw a string of Hawks goals – Rough for his fourth, Gunston, Simpkin and Smith – giving us a handsome 37-point lead at the final break.

BOOOOOOOO!

The final quarter was largely uneventful once Hodge dribbled through the quarter's opening goal to establish a 40-plus-point lead.

Two noteworthy points, however: Hodge in particular, but really the entire team, exerted exceptional pressure (like having to write a really hard essay) and created multiple turnovers through smothers or interceptions. Also, with each free kick to Hawthorn (and admittedly, we did receive a few), the booing extended from Burgoyne to the umpires, to such a degree that it almost became white noise. I thought the umpires' only chance of survival might be to join Julian Assange and seek asylum in Ecuador.

Savage kicked our nineteenth and final goal for the match after a strong mark 50 metres out. This was his third, to go with Smith's three and Gunston's and Roughead's bags of five each. Our 45-point victory was fairly convincing and gave predictable rise to chatter about us being better, or at least as good, without Buddy. Seriously, what nonsense. If you lined up the Hawthorn team and went pick for pick, as per the longstanding school selection formula, Buddy would be picked among the top four (with Hodge, Mitchell and Roughead) every time. To suggest that we'd be better off without Buddy was like saying that Monet's oeuvre would be better off without waterlilies.

Final scores: Hawthorn 19.10.124 d Port Adelaide 12.7.79
Ladder Position: 1st
What we learned: At the NGV I read with interest the plaque explaining that, late in his life, Monet suffered from cataracts that affected his ability to distinguish contrasting colours and filtered his vision through a yellow–brown film. Much like my own vision, really. I've been seeing life through a yellow–brown film for years. I thought this simply reflected my Hawthorn bias; I didn't realise it was a medical condition. Lucky one of our major sponsors is a health-care fund.
What we already knew: Hamish McLachlan doesn't get out much.

A TALE OF TWO TEAMS

I put in an extended session at the gym on Saturday morning, 20 July, not because I was pushing myself to new peaks, or rather troughs, of physical exertion, but because one of the televisions above the tread-mills was replaying a Hawthorn–Bulldogs fixture from a few years ago. It was early in the third and the scores were close when I climbed on the bike, so I had no choice but to stay until I found out the result.

First I had to try to work out when the match was played. The players provided the clues. Brent Renouf, Beau Muston and Wade Skipper were going around for the Hawks, while for the Dogs, Rocket Eade was in the box and Barry Hall, Brad Johnston and the bloke who wore number 1 and looked like Merlin from the TV series were all running around. Shaun Burgoyne's presence helped me establish that it was probably 2010, and I could then settle down to enjoy the match because I had a feeling that we'd won.

It was still tight at the final break, but spectacular goals from Mitchell and Hodge put us in front, then Buddy seemed to seal the deal with a trademark long goal from 50 out on the boundary. A late goal to the Dogs, however, after a baffling decision to pay 50 against Buddy (it was one of those games where the umpires devoted them-selves to penalising him) brought it back to within a goal. Our boys hung on heroically, but only just, for the ball was heading towards the Bulldogs' goal square when the siren sounded.

Watching this match caused me to reflect on the long history of memorable games between Hawthorn and Footscray/Western Bulldogs, and all those classic encounters over the years … and I realised, not without some degree of disquiet, that in fact there'd hardly been any. Both teams had joined the league 88 years ago, in 1925, yet in all that time they had barely played a significant match.

Okay, there'd been the 1961 Grand Final – our first flag, so quite significant – but there were very few other matches of any import that I could recall.

In 1984 Leigh Matthews played his 300th game and Michael Tuck his 250th on the same day at Western Oval. Then in 1985 the teams contested both the Qualifying and Preliminary Finals, the latter of which was Matthews's penultimate game, which he marked by coming from the bench to kick two goals and send us to the Grand Final.

In 2007 I recall Buddy kicking 2.11 at Docklands in a big Hawks win, and then in 2008 he kicked eight in the Qualifying Final, which the Hawks also won easily. The very next time we played them, however, in 2009, I watched in horror as the Hawks, reigning premiers by then, went in at half time trailing 13.10 to 0.4 – that's right, not a single goal in the first half.

Since then, there was the afternoon in 2010 when Jordan Lewis, running back with the flight of the ball, got knocked out by a jumping Jarrod Harbrow, who was also flying for the ball and collected Lewis in the head on his way through. Lewis didn't even get a free kick, despite the head supposedly being sacrosanct. Under the new rules it might actually be a free kick to Harbrow for having his legs taken from under him. But my memory of other momentous matches was as sketchy as Jordan Lewis's after that incident.

A TALE OF TWO KICKS

Of the aggregate 389 kicks recorded by Hawthorn and the Western Bulldogs during their Round 17 encounter, the match, having very little else to distinguish it, came to be defined by just two of them. One travelled approximately 70 metres and was a contender for goal of the year, and the other travelled just 10 metres and was a contender for miss of the year. Both kicks came from Hawthorn players and represented the yin and yang of Hawthorn.

The first kick by Luke Hodge was perhaps noteworthy as much for the way he gathered the ball as for the actual kick. Taking the ball from the centre stoppage, Bulldog Ryan Griffin turned on to his right and sunk his boot into it to send it forward, but succeeded in kicking it directly into the chest of the oncoming Hodge, who, without breaking stride, carried the ball for two or three steps before launching a massive kick that landed in an empty goal square and bounced through for a goal.

The second kick, from Kyle Cheney, was the result of a 50-metre penalty against the Bulldogs' Jordan Roughead (Jarryd's cousin), which put the man on the mark just five metres out, meaning that Cheney was kicking from the goal square. In a game where Hawthorn had already kicked inaccurately, Cheney set a new benchmark for waywardness, shanking it into the goal post.

Kyle is a name of Scottish origin meaning "strait", as in a narrow sea channel, not to be confused with its homophone "straight", as in direct, accurate kick from five metres out!

Of course, it was easy to laugh at a miss like this, but anyone who has ever lined up a "gimme" will know that it's not as easy as it looks, and that a goal square looms longer and larger in reality than it appears on TV when you've got to kick over a man on the mark.

To test the degree of difficulty of the kick, I took Oscar and a match-day Sherrin down to the local park. I planted myself on the mark five metres out and gave him 10 kicks to see how many he could kick accurately. I sledged, I jumped about waving my arms, I vilified him, I called his mother rude names, I questioned his patrimony (Hey, hold on – that's me!), but he still calmly slotted 10 out of 10. So perhaps it is as easy as it looks.

I considered conducting the same experiment with my 80-year-old mum to test the accuracy of the time-honoured sledge "My mother could kick that!", but her eyesight is going, affecting her balance, and she is walking with a limp, so I didn't want to be the agency of a terrible accident just for the sake of an experiment. The point being, however, that if a 13-year-old schoolboy could kick it, a 24-year-old professional footballer, even an ex-Melbourne player, should be able to. At least Kyle could now be teased for something other than his red hair.

In fairness, Kyle wasn't the only player to miss from the goal square. All up, I counted four other players in various circumstances. In the first quarter Gunston sprayed a hurried snap-shot, in the final quarter the Poo missed the ball entirely while attempting a kick off the ground, whereas for the Dogs, Koby Stevens missed in the second quarter and Liam Jones from off the ground in the third. It was just that sort of match.

The first quarter made for engaging and diverting viewing, with Hawthorn creating numerous and regular scoring opportunities. Although they didn't take all of them, you got a sense that eventually the sheer weight of numbers would result in an influx of goals.

But it didn't eventuate – not until the final quarter, at least. Over the course of the second and third quarters, both teams kicked just 3.6 each. Hodge's goal was the lone highlight of the second quarter, unless you counted Cheney's spectacular miss, and the third quarter was a dour, messy affair, with neither team making any progress. Hawks fans were keen to see how new boy Will Langford fared, but otherwise the action was as stagnant and frustrating as watching the Australian top order trying to eke out runs at Lord's, or the Australian government trying to cobble together a coherent asylum-seeker policy.

In the final quarter the match seemed to right itself, with Hawthorn running in four goals in five minutes through Lewis, the Poo and Simpkin (two) to get the lead out to 44 points, something like the margin we were anticipating. Then the Dogs threw in one last plot twist, kicking four goals in the final three minutes to bring the margin back to 19 points.

Overall, it was a game that lived up to the rich history between these two clubs.

Final scores: Hawthorn 13.17.95 d Western Bulldogs 11.10.76
Ladder position: 1st
What we learned: With the birth of the royal baby two days after the match, the Queen now had a full complement of heirs on the interchange bench: Charles, William and the baby Prince George, with Harry in the fluoro-green sub's vest.
What we already knew: That Channel 9 has no hypocrisy alarm. During the week, the *Mornings* team of Sonia Kruger and David Campbell previewed a segment critical of those who participate in "fat shaming", the practice of photographing larger people in humiliating poses and posting the pics on social media sites. Much tut-tutting then ensued. In the very next segment, however, Ken Sutcliffe joined them and discussed the streaker in the previous night's State of Origin rugby league clash, joking about his size and suggesting you could sell advertising space on his generous girth. Hello? Fat shaming, anyone? It must be acceptable to do it on national television, just not online.

Everything old is new again: It was good to see that the Western Bulldogs had re-adopted the former jumper they had worn for the bulk of the previous century – from 1901 to 1975. The classic royal blue with one red and one white horizontal band looked stylish, even groovy. Much better without that stylised bulldog head, which looked like a car manufacturer's emblem. I've also heard, they're considering reverting to the name Footscray. I was pleased in 2006 when Hawthorn re-adopted the brown stripes on the back with the black number on a white panel, as they'd worn when I was young. It is unlikely, however, that we'll replace "Hawks" with our original emblem, "Mayblooms", anytime soon. If nothing else, September blooms are preferable.

Another cause for nostalgic celebration was the name Langford appearing in the Hawthorn line-up. There are many areas of subjective dispute in football – which is the greatest team of all time: Collingwood in the 1920s–30s, Melbourne in the '50s, Carlton from 1979–82, Hawthorn in the '80s, Brisbane 2001–04 or the current Geelong team. But one thing on which everyone agrees is that Chris Langford, that chiselled-jawed Adonis with the cleft in his chin, is the most handsome man ever to play AFL football.

Langford was the champion full-back during the great Hawthorn era of the '80s, playing in four premiership sides, and is now an AFL administrator. So it was particularly gratifying to see his son, Will Langford, take his place in the Hawthorn colours.

NOW IS THE WINTER OF OUR CONTENT

The TV previews of Friday night's top-of-the-table clash between Hawthorn and Essendon naturally focused on their many famous encounters from the '80s, when, over the course of four or more years, both teams traded not only top spot on the ladder but also a series of blows. Predictably, the emphasis in this coverage was skewed towards those occasions when individual players – or, on some occasions, the entire two teams – brawled it out.

Throughout the week I saw regular replays of the all-in brawl of the 1985 Grand Final, in which Dermott Brereton and Leigh Matthews played starring roles for Hawthorn. I saw footage of Brereton kissing Essendon's Billy Duckworth and then running though the Essendon huddle at Waverley Park. Plus there was Brereton's hip and shoulder that knocked out Paul Van Der Haar in the 1989 Second Semi Final. Naturally, the "line in the sand" game of 2004 was also featured, when Dermott Brereton, by then a board member, allegedly spoke to the team at half time and exhorted them not to take a backward step, to draw a line in the sand and no longer accept Essendon's easy dominance over them. The vision of Richie Vandenberg hurling himself at Essendon players is probably the reason he was appointed captain a few years later.

The attentive reader will have noticed that one name is recurring in these scenarios, illustrating what a commanding figure Brereton was in forging this rivalry between Hawthorn and Essendon. It's impressive that he was still figuring strongly more than 10 years after he'd last played for Hawthorn. Hawks fans of a certain age tend to revere Brereton in a manner similar to how ALP voters revere Paul Keating – with a sort of misty-eyed hero worship.

Similar, perhaps, to how Essendon fans might revere Matthew Lloyd, an astute observer of the game who provided the most recent instalment to the well-worn sequence of brawling footage when he ironed out Brad Sewell in 2009.

Rather than focus on past brawls between the two teams, it would have been more appropriate to show footage of an Essendon board meeting, where they were going at one another with all the ferocity of Brereton and Duckworth. Watching Essendon unravel and tear one another apart over the ongoing supplements saga was one of the more enjoyable aspects of an otherwise uneventful season – the cause of much Hawk content.

In casting about for parallels of this saga, I'm reminded most of Shakespeare's Richard III, which opens with Richard saying, "Now is the winter of our discontent ..." – a phrase which you suspect might have been minuted once or twice in 2013 during Essendon board meetings.

In the course of the play, Richard uses a mix of evil and Machiavellian cunning, firstly to take the throne and then to keep it. He dispatches those who stand in his way, double-crosses those he employs to do his dirty work and disposes of those who pose an ongoing threat ... Hmmm, remind you of anyone?

A quick list of Richard's victims during the play includes: King Henry VI (stabbed); Edward, elder Prince of Wales (stabbed); George, Duke of Clarence (assassinated by hitmen hired by Richard);

the two hitmen themselves (missing, presumed murdered); King Edward IV (dies of broken heart over Richard's machinations); the two baby princes (smothered to death in the Tower); Hastings (beheaded); Buckingham, Rivers, Gray and Vaughan (executed); and George Stanley (assassinated). Replace these names with Matthew Knights, Dean Robinson, Stephen Dank, Paul Hamilton, Ian Robson, Elizabeth Lukin and David Evans, and suddenly the body count at Windy Hill begins to resemble Richard's own at court.

As Richard is taken down in the final battle and lays asprawl in imminent defeat, his throne taken, he bellows the famous lament: "A horse! A horse! My kingdom for a horse!" How James Hird would benefit from the sudden emergence of a noble white steed is less clear, especially as he was showing no signs that he might ride off quietly into the sunset.

As Richard observes:

Conscience is but a word that cowards use,
Devis'd at first to keep the strong in awe:
Our strong arms be our conscience, swords our law.
March on, join bravely, let us to't pell-mell;
If not to heaven, then hand in hand to hell.

And then, finally, once banished to the bottom of the ladder – or "hell" as Richard terms it – Essendon's winter of discontent will become glorious summer for the sons of Hawks.

YOU'LL NEVER WALK ALONE WITH LIVERPOOL ... BUT YOU CAN FORGET ABOUT SITTING TOGETHER AT ETIHAD

More than 95,000 people crammed into the MCG midweek to watch Liverpool and Melbourne Victory – two middling teams in their respective leagues – play a practice match. Imagine how many people, the top two teams in the AFL, Hawthorn and Essendon, might therefore be expected to draw for a Friday-night clash.

Well, barely half that, as it happened, but this didn't reflect a code defection or lack of interest on the part of Melbourne's footy public, rather the decision to play this game at Etihad Stadium, a venue that only holds 53,359 and then appears not to make all of those seats available.

More than a week before the match I tried without success to get tickets for me, Chan-Tha and Pete through any of the ticketing categories to which we were eligible: MCC members in Axcess One – no availability; Hawthorn members – only single seats; general public – no availability. We tried online and by phone and were told by the ticketing agency that there were no seats available. Despite this, when watching the telecast, there were plenty of empty seats at the ground and a crowd of 49,905, which by my calculations meant there were, in fact, 4454 seats available. We only wanted three.

When the AFL talks about protecting the code from the threat posed by soccer and rugby, they might want to look at how they schedule games and how tickets are sold (or not, as it happens) for Etihad.

IN: FRANKLIN, MITCHELL

As a result of not being able to secure tickets, we congregated at the newly reopened Duke of Wellington Hotel, on the corner of Flinders and Russell Streets.

The Duke of Wellington is named after the brave and honourable English general who defeated the evil and deceitful Napoleon – so the parallels were obvious and we went with the confidence that Essendon would face their Waterloo on the night.

One reason for confidence was revealed at team selection. Out: Cheney, Langford. In: Franklin, Mitchell. Not to be unfair to Cheney or Langford, but rarely had there been a more definitive or contrasting out/in combo. Cheney, who the previous week couldn't kick a goal from 10 metres, compared to Franklin, a two-time Coleman medallist who kicked 100 in a season; and Langford, who had played one game for four possessions, compared to Mitchell, who had played 236 games and averaged around 30 possessions a match. That was about an eight-goal improvement on the previous week's side alone, before they even took the field. In political terms, it was a bit like replacing Howard and Abbott with Mandela and Gandhi.

There were early setbacks – and I'm not referring to Essendon's two early goals, but the price of the drinks. A 330 ml stubby of Hawthorn Pilsner (what else would you drink on this night?) cost $12 at the Duke. That's fine if you're on Buddy's reputed salary, but for those of us on a more modest contract, it's ridiculous. It's brewed about five kilometres up the road so it's not as if there's excessive transport costs involved. On a dollar per millilitre matrix, that possibly comes in as more expensive than Veuve Clicquot.

Having said that, it was nice to clink a "Hawthorn" when Lewis answered with a nice snap to kick our first. I haven't checked the stats, but I have a gut feeling we win when Lewis kicks our first.

And we probably also usually win when Buddy snags three in the opening quarter. After his first, Jake Carlisle elbowed him from behind to take him down, and yet seemed a little put out when Buddy retaliated. Roughing up Buddy can put him off his game sometimes, but you have to be tougher and better than Carlisle.

Number 38 for Essendon, Nick Kommor, was also trying to sling people around when they didn't have the ball – in the first quarter it was Guerra and in the second, Hodge. In the third quarter he slung Isaac Smith into the fence, and then tried to punch on with Brendan Whitecross, while in the final quarter he tried it on with Taylor Duryea. He was acting very tough for a running player who had *three*, count them, *three* kicks for the match – and one of them was penalised for "deliberate out of bounds". In years past you might have suggested he was on the angry pills, but of course such a suggestion might seem a bit loaded at Essendon these days – after all, it might be right! For a team that had been accused of taking anti-obesity drugs, they were certainly still trying to throw some weight around.

After trailing four goals to two halfway through the first term, the Hawks kicked the next four in the first quarter and eight of the next nine by half time, giving them an unassailable 32-point lead. And it was unassailable because they were playing with utter ruthlessness. There was no way Essendon was going to get back into it.

Essendon's only goal in this period was the first of the second quarter to Michael Hurley, and even then he was the beneficiary of a lucky bounce after a Hawthorn smother. At that point there was 9:30 left to run in the second quarter and the Hawks led by just 10 points. Just over three minutes later, with 6:02 left to run, the Hawks had added four goals and led by 31 points.

Firstly, Cyril got it from Breust in the centre, and he ran and goaled from 60. Then Rough won a tough one-on-one and grubbered one through. A minute later Buddy wheeled around, avoided two tacklers and slotted it from 50. The Poo got one a minute later after a period of intense Hawthorn play.

The third quarter continued in a similar vein, with Hawthorn dominating after Essendon started well. Goals to Lewis and the Poo were followed by one to Hale after a relayed free kick when Roughead went down. Rough was shepherding and got elbowed in the head, but despite him being the one who was hit, Essendon fans booed him for the rest of the match. Go figure.

The match was over as a contest by this stage, particularly after Hodge intercepted a handball at half back that resulted in Buddy's fifth goal at the other end a moment later. Buddy added three more in the final quarter for a total of eight, and Breust two, taking the margin up to 10 goals and adding another happy chapter to Buddy's domination of Essendon. There were quite a few more empty seats by the time the siren rang.

This was an impressive performance by the Hawks – our most complete since we played Sydney earlier in the year. We played with confidence and daring and maintained precision and pressure for the entire match. It was a promising sign of what Hawthorn can do when it really matters. It was just a shame there weren't more people there to see it.

Final scores: Hawthorn 22.11.143 d Essendon 13.9.87

Ladder position: 1st

What we learned: That Essendon fans were either delusional or their grasp of right and wrong was the reverse of reality. They booed Roughead after an Essendon player elbowed him in the head to knock him out, yet continued to gather at press conferences to cheer on James Hird, whose controversial coaching regime was threatening to destabilise their club.

What we already knew: That Buddy relishes demoralising Essendon as much as any Hawks fan – eight goals in this match, two previous bags of nine, plus the two famous running goals at the MCG in 2010. Who said we didn't need him?

What we were still trying to work out: Gary Ablett Jr of the Gold Coast Suns played his 248th league game against Carlton in Round 18 – the same number of games as his famous father played. This fuelled much debate about who is the best Ablett. Predictably, most people over the age of 40 nominated Gary Sr, and most people under the age of 40 nominated Gary Jr.

I would nominate Geoff, Gary Sr's older brother. Geoff Ablett played 202 games for Hawthorn, including premierships in 1976 and 1978. Not only that, he also won the first three Grand Final half-time sprints from 1979–81, representing Hawthorn, and a fourth for St Kilda in 1985. It should be noted that neither Gary Sr or Jr has won the half-time sprint.

The Coleman Medal: The award for the leading goal-kicker in the AFL is named after an Essendon full forward, John Coleman, who kicked 537 goals in a fleeting career. It was perhaps fitting that, with his eight goals against the Bombers, Buddy Franklin should come back into the fray to win his third medal. He was on 46 goals, just eight behind joint leaders Josh Kennedy of the Eagles and the great Jarryd Roughead, both on 54. Roughead was having a remarkable year, and I was banking on him and Buddy to go one/two in the Coleman – I wasn't bothered in which order they finished.

A HARD RAIN'S A-GONNA FALL

During the third quarter of the Saturday-afternoon match, the live weather radar was beamed from the giant scoreboard, accompanied by an announcement that a big storm was on its way and that patrons should make their way under cover. It wasn't quite "Run for your lives!" but it wasn't that far from it.

I was there with Oscar and Chan-Tha as usual, but also my brother Graeme, who barracks for the Tigers, and his son Max. We heeded the advice and scurried to higher ground on level four, but with nowhere else to go for shelter, the Hawthorn players retreated into themselves, or just got spooked. Some must even have taken the ground announcer's advice and gone down into the rooms, given that we didn't see them in the action for the rest of the match. As in the corresponding match last season, we were completely overrun by Richmond, which from that moment kicked eight of the next 10 goals to run out easy winners.

After producing one of our best performances of the season the previous week against Essendon, it was somewhat disappointing and unexpected that we'd follow it up with one of our worst. It was like when Oasis released *Be Here Now* as the follow-up to *Morning Glory*.

LOSING THE PLOT

"Happy families are all alike; every unhappy family is unhappy in its own way." Thus Tolstoy begins *Anna Karenina*, introducing us to the troubled Oblonsky family. Equally, though, he could be referring to Hawthorn – the Family Club – and, footy fans in general. Fans of winning teams are all alike, grinning manically and chanting cheerily over their team's triumphs, while fans of losing teams, such as Hawthorn this particular week, all find their own way to be unhappy, each attributing blame to a different cause.

For some it's injuries: Birchall and Shiels still missing and Max Bailey replaced in the selected side by debutant Jon Ceglar. For others it's the umpires, and in this match you didn't need to run a forensic eye over the game to find several decisive howlers, although admittedly we were the beneficiaries of as many as Richmond. For some it's the forward line, with Buddy, Roughead, Breust and Gunston kicking only one goal between them.

Of course, I blame the weather and therefore climate change, and hence successive Australian governments for not acting sooner. The carbon tax had been active for 13 months yet we were still getting these extreme weather events. Hawthorn's elite professionals shouldn't have to play in these conditions. Perhaps we should put a roof on the G?

HARD RAIN

The match began well enough: after Jack Riewoldt kicked the first for Richmond, Buddy kicked one for us, followed by Lewis. Riewoldt kicked his second, which was answered by Buddy taking a nice grab. Hopes of a shootout between two of the competition's best goal kickers soon dissipated, however, as Buddy's shot went sailing out on the full.

And from there it was all Richmond: they continually won the ball and moved it quickly and accurately, adding four more goals to take a three-goal lead to the break. At quarter time the clearances were 16–2 in Richmond's favour and the only surprise was that we weren't further behind.

Hawthorn played it tough and tight in the second quarter, stemming the flow and adding three goals while keeping Richmond goal-less. The inaccuracy continued, with Hale and Gunston both hitting the post, but finally Guerra, playing his 250th match, put us in front at the 27-minute mark. From there I thought we'd gradually edge further ahead, with those players who hadn't been able to get into the match – Roughead, Rioli, Gunston et al. – taking over.

A miss to Buddy on the siren and another to Burgoyne not long after the restart, however, sapped any momentum we might have been building and undermined the advantage which players like Smith and Mitchell had worked hard to build up. Even when new boy Ceglar marked strongly and goaled, our quarter and a bit of near dominance had yielded just a nine-point advantage.

When the rains hit, Hawthorn continued to play a quaint possession game built on precise passing, which is fine if you're moving goalwards, but winning the uncontested possession count doesn't mean much if you can't clear the half-back line.

Richmond, on the other hand, played a more dynamic game that involved winning the ball – usually through skipper Trent Cotchin – and getting it out to its runners, who continued to surge forward. The inevitable goals ensued.

My brother, of course, relished the second-half onslaught and delighted in winning his bets with Max and Oscar and shouting out the "Yellow and black!" refrain in the Richmond theme song. As a Richmond fan, however, he has to be a realist. He knows not to rub it in too hard, because he's aware that any given Richmond triumph is concluded

only ever the precursor to their next embarrassing loss. He knows that even though this win kept Richmond in seventh position on the ladder, with a three-game buffer to the ninth-placed side, there were still four rounds to go, and if any team was capable of blowing a finals appearance from this position, it was Richmond.

It was only our third loss for the season, so perhaps it would be overreacting to read too much into it or assign it too much significance. Yet with the skies darkening, the wind blustering, the rain tumbling down in sheets, and the ground announcer's ominous storm warning, it was difficult not to think of Bob Dylan's early song "A Hard Rain's a-Gonna Fall", in which a young man returning from his travels is questioned as to where he's been, what he's seen, what he's heard and so on. Over five long verses, the blue-eyed son recounts the apocalyptic visions and portents that assailed him on his journey and predicts heavy precipitation, which, in the context of the song, might be read as the end of the world.

Hawks fans perhaps felt something of this at the end of the day. We'd been drenched, flicked with the corners of Richmond flags, stuck next to rabid Tigers' fans and had wandered lost and disorientated in Tigerland.

We'd seen Jack Riewoldt mark in front of Gibbo; Brett Deledio and Dustin Martin break clear from packs; Buddy and Burgoyne miss key shots from 30 metres out; and Daniel Jackson slot one from the boundary.

We'd heard the Tigers fans roar home their goals, our shouts for "Ball!" go unanswered, the siren that signals the end, and the Tigers fans shouting "Yellow and black!"

All in all, it was an unpleasant afternoon at the football, but we were still on top of the ladder; the sun, although somewhat pallidly, shone the next day; and we had St Kilda to look forward to the following week.

Final scores: Richmond 16.11.107 d Hawthorn 9.12.66
Ladder position: 1st^t
What we learned: A shot of Dermott Brereton and Jason Dunstall
together in the Fox commentary box was flashed on the big
screen to remind us ever so gently of the good old days. Much
was made of the fact that Richmond had now defeated Hawthorn in two consecutive matches. Some were even calling it a
streak, but I prefer my streaks a tad longer, like the one that
spanned almost the entire length of Dermie and Dunstall's
playing days together, when Hawthorn defeated Richmond in
16 consecutive matches over 10 years from Round 16, 1985, to
Round 21, 1994.

The only occasion I can find when Richmond defeated
Hawthorn in a match with both Dermie and Dunstall playing
was Round 5, 1985, Dunstall's first year at Hawthorn. That day
Dermie kicked 6.1 and Dunstall 1.5.

The streak was finally broken at Waverley Park in Round
3, 1995, after Dermie had left Hawthorn, when Richmond
kicked 4.16 to Hawthorn's 5.4 to win by six points – but even
then we kicked one more goal than them.

What we already knew: A series of baffling free kicks both ways
suggested the umpires could easily find a role officiating in one
of the Ashes Tests underway simultaneously in England.
Thank God there's no DRS in AFL. Oh, wait, there is.

What we'll never forget – even though we didn't see it: Hawthorn's
long-running winning streak against Richmond included a
match in Round 7, 1992, when Jason Dunstall kicked 17.5. I wasn't
there that day, unfortunately. Instead of watching a historical
record-breaking feat of goal-kicking prowess, I was watching
my partner and eventual wife graduate at Melbourne University.

So, rather than a procession of Dunstall goals, I sat through a somewhat less dynamic procession of vice chancellors, deans, professors and other assorted academics in ceremonial garb. When Dunstall kicked his 100th goal later in the season, one of my friends suggested that I shouldn't jump the fence for the traditional ground invasion as I'd only seen 83 of them.

WALK A MILE IN BUDDY'S SHOES

ROUND 20 – ST KILDA V HAWTHORN
Etihad Stadium, Friday 9 August 2013

Hawthorn had been using Buddy for six years to sell memberships and promote the club, so it was only fair that Buddy use Hawthorn to promote his new "Buddy boots".

Breaking his six-month silence on his contract negotiations and using the launch of his new range of footwear to announce that he wanted to stay at Hawthorn may not have shed any real light on his intentions for the next season, but it certainly guaranteed that his product launch made the news on every TV channel and other associated media outlet.

As free advertising stunts go, it was straight from the manual: make an ad newsworthy and save on marketing costs.

And just to ensure all angles were covered, Buddy's occasional confidant and current Ashes combatant Kevin Pietersen also got tweeting about the boots. That made the news too.

Perhaps if Buddy had been able to convince James Hird to say he'd drunk AOD-9604 from the Buddy boot and got a heckler to hurl one at Kevin Rudd during the leaders' debate, he'd have achieved saturation coverage – and possibly hero status if the shoe hit.

In the end, Buddy didn't play in the match against St Kilda, which gave him a chance to do a half-time interview on Channel 7, where, guess what, he was able to spruik his boots again. It was what Tom Waterhouse might call an "embedded" commercial.

So, as far as we were concerned, all power to Buddy and long may we walk a mile in his shoes, or Buddy boots – or, as Amy Winehouse called them, her "Fuck me pumps".

But then we'd have bought the Buddy boots anyway, to go with our Nena + Pasadena T-shirts. We were just waiting on his line of fragrances and lingerie. I'm not joking – I drank "Hawthorn" beer from a Buddy stubby holder; why wouldn't I have sprayed on "Buddy Odour" deodorant and worn "Buddy Briefs" underwear? (Hey, Buddy – those names are trademarked, okay?)

ROCK THE WHITTEN BAR

It's fair to say that without Buddy, the match lost a bit of its cachet, notwithstanding the insight-less Channel 7 half-time interview.

There's not too much to really say about the night: it was tight and crowded in close early and there was a fair bit of niggle, although even this better describes the bar area at the Nixon Hotel beforehand than the game itself.

Most post-match reports about the game suggest it was a dour and boring affair, only marginally less dull and predictable than the Kevin Rudd and Tony Abbott leaders' debate. Some even found it more harrowing than Patrick's death on *Offspring* the week previous, while others were so lulled into a comatose state that they turned over to the Fourth Test looking for sporting action.

I was at the match with Chan-Tha. As it was Friday night, the match served as a backdrop for after-work drinks, and to that end it was fine. The Hawks were expected to win comfortably and did so, leaving Chan-Tha and me plenty of time to socialise with friends in a series of bars on level two, from Axcess One, the E.J. Whitten Bar and eventually the Medallion Club, where we saw out the game.

True, it wasn't one of the classics, as I discovered when I watched it back, but that's not to say it compares to the infamous match between these two teams from 2007, which then Hawthorn president Jeff Kennett called "appalling" and Nick Riewoldt labelled the "shame game". That match is widely regarded as the worst match ever, with both teams adopting a defensive game plan that meant there was hardly any scoring. Still, Hawthorn won on that occasion so I wasn't overly bothered.

This was a veritable goal feast compared to that match. Even so, it was the sort of game that the app Snapchat was designed for: short one- to 10-second grabs that are automatically deleted. Okay, so Snapchat was mainly invented for sexting, but that isn't to say it doesn't have other applications, like footy matches with five or so separate moments that might be constructed into highlights worth posting to someone. (You have to wonder how it is that staff for the former US congressman and New York City mayoral candidate Anthony Weiner never told him about a sexting app that deleted the evidence.)

But the match had its highlights: we won the very first centre clearance, which, after the previous week, was something to celebrate. Sewell took it from the bounce and fired it to our much-heralded multi-pronged, über-forwards ... um, Matt Spangher and Sam Grimley. They were perhaps unlikely targets on our forward line, but as we'd only kicked nine goals the previous week, perhaps Clarko was making a point.

For the second consecutive week, Cyril seemed a bit off the pace, so much so that by the second quarter on the telecast, Bruce McAvaney observed that he looked a bit "wider in the hips" – they were Bruce's exact words. Talk about how to give a bloke body issues. If Cyril is "wide in the hips", what does that make Stuart Dew?

Rough was also evidently bored and decided to take matters into his own hands, grabbing a spilt ball and storming into goal for his second. Gunston slotted a nice set shot and Spangher kicked one off the ground. A 5.10 quarter was wasteful, but still set up a reasonably good half-time lead.

For the third quarter Chan-Tha and I had migrated to the E.J. Whitten Bar, which is behind glass on level two behind the goals. I don't know which end; I can't tell the two ends apart at Etihad – not until they change the names from the "Lockett" and "Coventry" ends to the "Dunstall" and "Hudson" ends will I bother to work it out. It wasn't an ideal location because I couldn't really see much, but there was one highlight. Rough took a kick from the goal square, but the first I knew of it was when the ball thundered into the glass right next to me. It was so close I could clearly read the word SHERRIN. It was equally exhilarating and a bit of a shock to see the ball that had just come off Rough's toe so close. I felt as the Navy Seals must have when they turned a corner and found Osama bin Laden right in front of them. Okay, perhaps that's stretching it.

Isaac Smith also kicked a nice long goal in the third, but that was about it. Likewise for the final quarter: Breust took a nice strong one-handed, not-looking mark and goaled, but on the whole it wasn't a classic encounter. Even so, it was more inspiring than the week's debate between prime ministerial aspirants Kevin Rudd and Tony Abbott.

It's worth noting, however, that for a number of weeks Smith, Stratton, Puopolo and Savage had been among our best players. And Savage finally had a haircut that lived up to his name; he looked like Joe Strummer from "Rock the Casbah"-era Clash.

HAWTHORN AND ST KILDA THROUGH THE AGES

It was not the worst Hawthorn v St Kilda game ever – as I mentioned, that honour belongs to the "shame game" from May 2007. Nor was it the best: think the 1971 Second Semi or Grand Final, both thrillers, both narrow Hawthorn victories, with the Grand Final regarded as one of the toughest matches ever.

Nor even the most remarkable: some will recall Princes Park in 1977 when Hawthorn kicked 41 behinds – winning 25.41.191 to 16.7.103, which remains a record for the most behinds in a match. Under cover of night the following week, maddened Hawks fans climbed the fence at Glenferrie Oval and chopped down the point posts. One dreads to think what we might have kicked had Buddy been at full forward that afternoon.

Then there was the 1999 clash at Waverley, when the Hawks overhauled a 53-point deficit midway through the second quarter to win by 13 points, in what was then a record comeback.

If this reads like a litany of Hawthorn triumphs, it simply echoes the long dominance we enjoyed over St Kilda in the '80s, as both sides hovered at opposing ends of the ladder. Between Round 12, 1979, and Round 22, 1989, Hawthorn strung together 20 consecutive wins over the Saints, finally losing by just three points in May 1990 at Moorabbin (when Russell Morris – then a Hawk – missed a shot in the final seconds). This winning streak was, and may still be, a record for one club over another.

Hawthorn and St Kilda share a rich and storied past as well as a few personalities, most famously Allan Jeans, who coached St Kilda to its only premiership in 1966, and then coached Hawthorn to three in the '80s. Among the players to have worn both the brown and gold stripes and the St Kilda tri-colour are Peter Everitt, Russell Greene, Russell Morris, Stuart Trott and Brent Guerra.

So there's as much that unites these two teams as sets them apart, but I was happy we found early separation from them and maintained a comfortable lead so that our Friday-night drinks could continue stress-free.

Final scores: Hawthorn 14.18.102 d St Kilda 7.14.56

Ladder position: 1st

What we learned: That being a person of momentary interest to the media is the same as having your country stolen, your culture desecrated and your people slain and disbanded. Speaking at a lunch before the Sydney v Collingwood match, Eddie McGuire said the "absolute injustice" he felt at being "done over by the media" (he said that without any irony?) gave him insight into the daily life of indigenous people in Australia. Now, I'm sure he meant to simply express something like empathy and understanding, but you can see how it might be misinterpreted. It might have been better if he'd simply expressed his regret for earlier in the year and got on with bagging Sydney's cost-of-living allowance.

What we already knew: Essendon and four of its henchmen – James Hird, Danny Cochoran, Mark Thompson and Dr Bruce Reid – have been charged with bringing the game into disrepute. Really, what's new? Essendon has been bringing the game into disrepute for over 100 years. As the AFL weigh up appropriate penalties, they might consider taking up Tony Wilson's idea, posted on Twitter, that Essendon's points from 1984 and 1985 should be wiped. Obviously, the premierships from those years would revert to Hawthorn. But if the AFL wants to think outside suspensions and premiership points penalties, given that actual evidence seems a little sketchy, I recommend they play on Essendon's refusal to adopt a clash strip and threaten them with a clash strip designed by Jacobim Mugatu from *Zoolander*.

Coleman watch: Rough played another great game, kicking five goals. This keeps him in the leading group for the Coleman Medal with 59 goals for the season, just one behind Josh

Kennedy of the Eagles. We need a big finish from Rough. With Hawthorn players only rarely winning the Brownlow Medal, I consider the Coleman to be the award that counts. In my lifetime it has been draped around a number of Hawthorn necks: John Peck (three times), Peter Hudson (four times), Leigh Matthews, Jason Dunstall (three times) and Lance Franklin (two times). Regardless of his great season, we know Rough won't win the Brownlow, so the Coleman would be an attractive accessory for him to wear on formal occasions.

BLOWIN' IN THE WIND

Surely every footballer's dream is to one day be able to say, "I pin-pointed Buddy with a lace-out pass 30 metres from goal in front of more than 70,000 people at the G." Well, Tyson Goldsack can now legitimately make this boast to his children and his grandchildren; the fact that he did it while playing for the opposition is the part of the story he might want to omit, or conceal in the footnotes.

It came courtesy of a botched kick-in that shanked off his boot and went straight to Buddy, who was "guarding space", as they say, 30 metres from goal. Buddy went back, ran around on his natural arc to allow for the wind, banged it on his boot and duly slotted his fourth for the night – and, according to Bruce McAvaney, his 300th overall at the MCG. This gave us a 26-point lead midway through the third quarter, sapped any shred of belief left in Collingwood, and perhaps made Collingwood captain Nick Maxwell wish he hadn't given Buddy a mouthful at half time.

THE ANSWER, MY FRIEND, IS BLOWIN' IN THE WIND ...

Two weeks previously, when Hawthorn lost to Richmond in the midst of dire storm warnings, I turned to Bob Dylan's apocalyptic fable "A Hard

Rain's a-Gonna Fall" to help me try to understand what had occurred.

This match against Collingwood was played in wild, blustery conditions that also brought to mind an early Dylan song, "Blowin' in the Wind", in which the young singer, seeking some sort of transcendence, poses a series of philosophical questions to try to explain the human condition and locate meaning in the universe. The answer to these questions, the song asserts, is blowing in the wind.

If this is true, there's a fair chance "the answer" was swirling and gusting about with the chip packets, pie wrappers, deflated thunder sticks and other assorted debris at the MCG on Friday night. The squall was such that if you had turned the MCG light towers into wind turbines you could have generated enough energy to power Victoria for the next decade.

Is it coincidence, or is Bob just prescient? The first hint that cosmic riddles would be solved came when Lewis marked 30 out and kicked our first goal, always a happy portent.

But "the answer" was also evident in several other acts throughout the night. In the first quarter you only had to look to Cyril's two-touch soccer goal, the first touch taking the ball out of Scott Pendlebury's lunging reach and the second touch hammering it into the back of the net. The answer was also evident when Buddy and Smith both kicked truly from set shots, when Whitecross snapped it around his body for a goal and when Breust roved it from Roughead's deft tap to kick another. Perhaps the most resounding answer in the first quarter came with Collingwood's Travis Cloke shooting right on the siren from 15 metres and missing badly to the left.

LIFE, THE UNIVERSE AND EVERYTHING

Sewell started well, having 13 disposals in the first quarter, as did Hale, who won the ball and had three shots on goal – they all missed but it gave Collingwood someone other than Buddy and Rough to worry about. Birchall was showing in his first game back from the knee injury he received against the Eagles in Round 13 that he hadn't lost his touch, and Gibbo, as ever, was strong in defence.

Douglas Adams reveals in his *Hitchhiker's Guide to the Galaxy* series that the answer to Life, the Universe and Everything is 42, which, strangely enough, is also the sum of Sewell (12), Hale (10), Birchall (14), and Gibbo's (6) jumper numbers. Am I stretching the point or is that just spooky?

In the second quarter you might have found "the answer" in Cyril's brilliant touch to set up two more goals: the first after taking three bounces to scoot away from the throng and fire a handball over the top to Smith in the goal square; the second when he somehow slid between Dane Swan and Ben Sinclair to fire a pass to Gunston directly in front.

The answer was also evident in Buddy receiving three free kicks in the space of three minutes – a sure sign there was some sort of enchantment in the air. An even clearer sign of paranormal activity was that he kicked two of them. The answer was blowing in the wind alright, and it was giving Buddy a helpful right-to-left fade on his kick.

THE MAX(WELL) FACTOR

All Buddy's free kicks were fairly clear, despite Collingwood fans booing (their default form of expression). It's still against the rules to simply charge someone who is going for a mark, as was the case with two of the decisions. In the case of the third free kick, it was hard to know exactly what Nick Maxwell was attempting to do – snuggle Buddy, perhaps (he's only human) – but whatever it was, it definitely wasn't going for the ball. Or perhaps the umpire had read recently retired Geelong defender Matthew Scarlett's book, *Hold the Line,* in which he labelled Maxwell as overrated and someone Geelong players didn't respect, and agreed.

Right on half time Buddy misfired a look-away handball, which Collingwood's Jarryd Blair intercepted; he goaled for Collingwood – their third in a matter of minutes – bringing the margin back to 15 points at the break. In his book, Matthew Scarlett revealed that his unflattering assessment of Nick Maxwell was based on an incident when Maxwell sledged Geelong players at three-quarter time in the 2010 Preliminary Final with Collingwood well ahead. In light of Scarlett's view, it was amusing to see Maxwell mouthing off in Buddy's face. Maxwell giving it to Buddy. Seriously? That would be the Buddy who had already kicked three goals, the Buddy who had single-handedly destroyed Collingwood on several occasions, the Buddy who leapt over players to kick a 75-metre goal in Round 3, the Buddy who, in my memory, Maxwell had never once dared to take as his primary opponent.

With three quick goals, and on the back of Quinten Lynch flattening Sam Mitchell from behind and well off the ball, the Collingwood players were full of huff and puff on the siren – pushing, shoving, mouthing off and jumper-punching. They swaggered off at half time, chests out, tatts glistening, full of bluster and belief. I mean, Quinten, Steele, Heath, Tyson and Travis may sound like they belong in a boy band, but these fellas are tough. We're just fortunate Clinton and Tarkyn weren't also playing.

FINDING ALL THE ANSWERS

So Collingwood came out for the third quarter fired up, fervent, spurred on and ready to roll ... and scrambled through just three behinds for the quarter.

Finding all the answers, the Hawks booted 3.4, including Buddy's goal from Goldsack's kick-in, plus another to Whitecross after Buddy won possession, wheeled around and onto his left, but instead of launching one of his long, curling shots on goal from 50, he speared a pass to Whitecross, who ran into an open goal. Beautiful! Nick Maxwell chose not to mouth off at this point.

In the final quarter, after a brief flurry from Collingwood, the answering goal came from Hill, and then Rough ended the argument with an emphatic kick from outside 50.

It was another great win for the Hawks, with Hodge, Whitecross and Smith among our best. Hang on, Hodge (15), Whitecross (11) and Smith (16); there's the answer to Life, the Universe and Everything again, 42. Can there be any lingering doubt that Hawthorn is central to some mysterious, overarching cosmic plan? Hawthorn is the answer.

Evoking Bob Dylan once again to illustrate a Hawthorn win may seem far-fetched and fanciful to some, but there is a long-standing connection between Dylan and Hawthorn. It goes right back to his 1965 album, *Highway 61 Revisited*, which, as the title shows, makes no secret that it's looking back at our first premiership, while his 1966 album, *Blonde on Blonde*, is a fairly clear reference to our recruiting policy of the mid-'90s.

RUNNETH OVER WITH BLUE CUPS

After the match Luke Hodge was presented with the Beyond Blue Cup, a trophy so named to help raise awareness about depression.

This complements the Blue Ribbon Cup we were awarded the previous week after defeating St Kilda, a trophy named in memory of police sergeants Gary Silk and Rodney Miller, who were killed in the line of duty.

And on Sunday, Aberfeldie's Under-14 Division 5 team – for whom my son Oscar plays, and who happen to wear jumpers with two blues – won their Grand Final in a stirring come-from-behind win. As great as Hawthorn's victory over Collingwood was, it was the boys wearing the Aberfeldie two-blue jumper who made the weekend a truly memorable one for football.

There is, however, one more cup to go ...

Final scores: Hawthorn 18.11.119 d Collingwood 12.12.84
Ladder position: 1st
What we learned: Well, the answer, my friend ... it's Hawthorn.
What we already knew: The goal-review system is being operated
by whichever video-illiterate third umpire is in charge of the remote control at the Ashes in England. How else to explain the fiasco in the second quarter that resulted in Taylor Duryea scoring the first rushed goal in AFL history?

The ball spilled in the goal square and Collingwood's Jarryd Blair flung his boot at it as Taylor Duryea dived to knock it through with his palm. The goal went for review, where it clearly showed Duryea tap it with an open palm over the line – it was so obvious they could nearly have paid a free against him for a deliberate behind. Blair's toe was nowhere near the ball – yet somehow this was called inconclusive. Even Chan-Tha, texting from San Francisco, could see that it was touched.
What we'd like to see: Bradley Manning, the soldier accused of
leaking classified material to WikiLeaks, announced after his trial concluded in the week following the Hawthorn–Collingwood match that he wanted to be known as Chelsea Manning and begin gender-transition treatment immediately. Deciding to change gender must require strength and conviction; it's nearly as radical as changing which team you support, or, indeed, which team you play for.

I may have joked about Clinton Young's decision to leave Hawthorn at the end of 2012 to join Collingwood. Changing stripes, quite literally. I could no sooner conceive of changing teams as I could of changing genders. Still, it is disappointing that Young hasn't played in either game against the Hawks this year, or in many games at all due to injury. As a member of Hawthorn's 2008 premiership team he is automatically elevated in my eyes to one of the Immortals, and I hope we'll see his booming left-foot kicks again in 2014 and beyond.

TRENDING NOW ... HAWTHORN

ROUND 22 — NORTH MELBOURNE V HAWTHORN
Etihad Stadium, Saturday 24 August 2013

Tracking pop-culture trends is the job of social ethnographers and train-spotters, with newspaper columnists usually following a year or so later. The very nature of the task means there's usually a lag time of some degree between a trend emerging and the same trend being recognised and widely acknowledged. Some argue that social-media forums have quickened the process dramatically and exponentially, but these are people whose idea of a cultural movement is something that stretches only as long as a hashtag compound or echoes as far as a retweet.

In the case of literary genres or schools of art, it can take years for the similarities and shared influences of individual practitioners to become apparent. Post-modernists and the Pre-Raphaelites had been at it for years before anyone noticed anything unusual. Not that anyone cared much even then.

In popular music, genres can be picked up much quicker, but even there, one singer in flared satin pants teamed with high-heeled boots does not glam rock make.

Broad cultural movements spanning a range of artistic endeavours or mediums can often take years to emerge, let alone be recognised and understood. Modernism, which began in the 1880s, didn't really get its name until well into the 1900s.

But there is a nascent movement now emerging across literature, music and football, which could well yet spread to other disciplines, other spectrums, until it defines life itself ... I speak, of course, of Hawthorn.

THE HAWTHORN RENAISSANCE

In 2012 I read a novel called *Eleven Seasons* by Paul D. Carter. It charts a young boy's journey through adolescence measured against eleven seasons following Hawthorn, encompassing the great '80s period.

More recently, I've been reading a novel called *The Whole of My World* by Nicole Hayes, published in early 2013. Another coming-of-age novel, this time about a teenage girl called Shelley who is obsessed by Hawthorn, or, as they are known in the book, Glenthorn, in probably the least convincing example ever of 'the names of some teams have been changed to protect their identities'.

The team are known as the Falcons, they wear brown and gold, they are based in a suburban ground in Leafy Crescent, which strongly resembles the Linda Crescent of Hawthorn's Glenferrie Oval, which is indeed leafy, and one of the cheer squad chants begins with "Give us an 'H'!" despite the team name beginning with a "G". Go on, literary trainspotters – knock yourselves out.

In *Eleven Seasons* the main character Jason Dalton is a young boy living with his mother, a sole parent. He goes to watch Hawthorn games with a schoolfriend at every opportunity. In *The Whole of My World*, Shelley is a young girl living with her father, also a sole parent. She takes herself off to watch Hawthorn games and training at every opportunity with a friend. It might just be that Hawthorn is the "family club", but you don't have to be Freud to work out that Hawthorn takes the role of surrogate parent in each case, even if they are different genders.

The Whole of My World is set in the '80s and I pick it as being set in set in 1984 – there is a reference to Hawthorn winning the premiership the previous year after a five-year drought (1978–83). Given that I was a prominent member of the Hawthorn Cheer Squad during this period, I read on with interest, thinking I might recognise a few people (especially given how poorly disguised the football team was). I was more than a little chuffed when, about 25 per cent of the way through (sorry, I can't give a page number; I was reading it on a Kindle), the leader of the cheer squad appears wearing pointy shoes, pants and a tweed jacket, rather than jeans and a footy jumper.

Of course, I never wore tweed back then, or indeed ever, but I certainly wore baggy pants, suit jackets and pointy shoes, so this character may indeed be loosely based on me, or an amalgam of me and other, much nicer people. This may well be my avatar, my debut as a literary character! Okay, so he's not quite Holden Caulfield or Stephen Dedalus, and sure, I'd have quite liked to have made my debut as a libertine or a master seducer in a work of erotic fiction (well, it would have to be fiction), but it's a start.

My chief criticism of *Eleven Seasons* was that there was too much focus on plot and character development at the expense of Hawthorn (including failing entirely to mention the 1989 Grand Final even though the book took place across that season). Of course, Mr Carter shouldn't be too angry; I'd make the same criticism of *Cloudstreet* or *The Tree of Man* – there's just not enough Hawthorn.

This criticism can't be levelled at *The Whole of My World*, at least up to the halfway mark, as Hawthorn is central to the action (even two of the teachers are known as Whitecross and Hodge), but I'm puzzled by the decision to disguise the true identity of the team, especially so transparently. Is it some post-modernist cypher? A comment about the nature of identity? Or some weird legal nicety?

In any case, I'll keep reading, if not to find out Shelley's dark secret (for, sure enough, there's one of those), but to see if, unlike the Hawks in 1984, the Mighty Falcons can pull off the big one!

These two novels carry explicit references to Hawthorn, and I'd say that together they constitute a new genre of literature (which will be supplemented by my own rollicking debut novel about a shortish, portly, balding 40-something who nominates for the AFL draft, gets picked up by Hawthorn and, through a bizarre chain of circumstance and against all the odds, kicks the winning goal after the siren to win the flag, all the while engaging in a torrid affair with Jaimee Rogers).

There are also books with less explicit references to Hawthorn the club, but which nonetheless can be considered as part of the genre – *Hawthorn and Child* by Keith Ridgway among them. Again, notice the parent–child relationship in the title. By subverting the style of title familiar to religious paintings of the Madonna and the baby Jesus, this book again casts Hawthorn as the surrogate parent, except in this case the parent of all humanity. Fair enough too.

The Hawthorn and Child of the title are not, in fact, parent and child, but two detectives. Hawthorn is a gay man who suffers from bad dreams and has a propensity for unexplained weeping – clearly a man haunted by the 2012 Grand Final loss.

It's perhaps fitting that, as the Melbourne Writers festival continued at Federation Square in August 2013, I'd unearthed a major new literary movement. But this genre is not confined to literature. In music, too, the Hawthorn motif is becoming prominent. Mayer Hawthorne is a singer, songwriter, multi-instrumentalist, producer et cetera, whose most recent album, *Where Does This Door Go*, was released to critical acclaim.

Likewise, Youngblood Hawke is an indie band that toured Australia with Pink, while New Zealand-born singer Ladyhawke also continues to grow in popularity.

This confluence of the "Hawthorn" and "Hawk" names across literature and music constitutes an emerging and powerful pop-culture movement – a renaissance, in fact, and one that will culminate, I predict, with another era of dominance in the AFL by Hawthorn.

TWERKING NOW ... HAWTHORN

Another recent trend in the world of what might be loosely called dance is that of "twerking". It's been around for a while but hit mainstream consciousness, thanks largely to Miley Cyrus's hit video "We Can't Stop" and her performance with Robin Thicke to his song "Blurred Lines" at the 2013 MTV Video Music Awards (VMAs).

Twerking is essentially a dance that involves sticking your arse out in a semi-squat and thrusting your hips back and forth in short, sharp movements, while shimmying your buttocks in a lewd and provocative manner. I'm unsure of the etymology of the word "twerking" – perhaps "sphinctering" might be a more accurate term to describe the dance – but you get the point.

Miley Cyrus sparked moral outrage with her performance at the VMAs, where she executed her now signature move of doubling over in front of Robin Thicke so that her arse jiggled and quivered at his crotch level. She did this while wearing a flesh-coloured bikini and, bizarrely, a giant Coles-ad hand with a prominent pointing finger. It's comforting to know that pop singers can still cause moral panic among the prudes and populists, and it reminded me of how Hawthorn approached their Round 22 match against North Melbourne.

Earlier in the year we defeated North by a few points, despite being largely outplayed for most of the match. A combination of North's poor kicking for goal and some Cyril magic got us over the line that evening.

Again in this match North completely outplayed us in the first half. Hard running, a bold, attacking game plan and good execution gave North an edge the Hawks found difficult to counter. North was winning it from the centre thanks to ruckman Todd Goldstein, spreading quickly and playing through Daniel Wells and Aaron Black, and they were kicking straight.

After Breust kicked the first goal of the match, North, through some sharp footy, banged on the next four. The Hawks looked flat-footed and slow by comparison, but thanks to some strong work by Buddy and Rough, we managed three goals towards the end of the quarter to even things up.

I was at the match with Oscar and Max, and we were sitting just behind the Hawthorn cheer squad, so we relished joining in the raucous barracking and chanting as the Hawks got going.

But our resurgence was only temporary, for in the second quarter North turned it on again. Goals to Ben Jacobs, Lindsay Thomas, Goldstein and Brent Harvey, who not only outbodied the much bigger Brian Lake to take a mark, but then ran around him to kick the goal and give North a 26-point lead. The North fans particularly loved that one. It was all looking a bit, well, ugly for the Hawks, particularly with Liam Shiels leaving the ground with an ankle injury and Hodge bleeding after receiving a cut to the head. But the second quarter finished like the first, with Buddy bagging a couple and Cyril and Breust each kicking one.

Thirteen points down at half time was a relatively good place to be, given how the two sides had played, and knowing that no one can blow a lead like North.

THE RIOLI QUARTET

So it was no surprise when the Hawks took over in the third, thanks largely to Cyril working his usual routine. After Roughead marked and goaled early, Cyril was pretty much responsible for the next four Hawthorn goals: kicking one himself after some artful twisting and dodging, then handballing over to Breust, who ran into an open goal, followed by some more elusive dodging to set up Bradley Hill and finally putting a pass into Hale's hands. It was pleasantly loud and boisterous where we were sitting. The "Hawthorn ... Hawthorn ... Hawthorn ... !" chant was going strong, and the goal surge had us standing and shouting as the ball flew towards us through the big sticks.

For the second time this season North had worked into a position where they looked like they might win, only to take their collective eyes off Cyril for long enough that he could steal it from under them.

It wasn't all Cyril, though: Max Bailey started to get on top of Goldstein, Mitchell went into the middle and won the ball, and Hodge – well, Hodge pretty much repelled every North forward thrust and reinforced why it's perfectly acceptable to have a man crush on him, even when he is wearing a bandage around his head.

Both teams missed opportunities in the final quarter, but goals to Rough and Buddy were enough to seal the match and condemn North to another narrow loss.

The thing about twerking is that it is a provocative tease in which the "twerker", if you will, assumes a vulnerable position while arousing their partner or antagonist and allowing them to feel dominant and in control. This is exactly the dance the Hawks have done in front of North twice this year – we've bent over in front of them, inviting dominance, teasing them with the illusion that they can take us, only to then slip away when they hesitated to act.

In addition to teasing, bending over in front of someone to present your arse has long been a sign of contempt or dismissal: mooning, for example. What we've done to North this season is exactly what Miley Cyrus did at the MTV awards – we at once teased them with the ridiculous hope of victory while also mooning them. Nice work, Hawks!

Final scores: Hawthorn 17.15.117 d North Melbourne 15.13.103
Ladder position: 1st
What we learned: North Melbourne is developing into a very good
team. Chairman James Brayshaw has steered them into a good
position off the field, and they have some exciting young
players on it. One of them, Aaron Black, looks like he'll be a
very good forward. He was selected with one of the draft picks
Hawthorn traded to get Josh Gibson from North. As good as
Black might become, getting Gibson to Hawthorn looks more
like a masterstroke each week. Along with Mitchell, he has
probably been our most consistent player in 2013. Plus by far
the coolest hipster in the side.

Shane Warne's transformation from bogan to bourgeois
goes beyond the luminous tan, weight loss and teeth whitening.
After England players were caught urinating on the Oval pitch
after the conclusion of the Fifth Test in London, Warne
labelled them "crass and arrogant". Warnie, that is, calling
England cricketers crass. Brilliant. You really know you've
gone off the rails if Warnie's giving you advice on etiquette,
deportment and humility.

What we already knew: The AFL would go soft on Essendon:
Hird banned for 12 months, the team kicked out of the finals, a
$2-million fine and the loss of draft picks for two years. Is that
all? Weak! I'd have liked to have seen more – the Coleman
Medal renamed the Hudson or Dunstall Medal, the team confined to the Big Brother house and Dermott Brereton
appointed to the board.

Essendon moaned about Andrew Demetriou hearing the
charges – they should be thankful it wasn't the US military tri-
bunal who sat in judgement of Bradley Manning, aka Chelsea
Manning. Or, worse, the *Age* editorial team.

On the day the penalties were handed out, the cover of *The Age* carried a full-colour photo of James Hird with the headline in large type, "BANNED", while in the top right-hand corner, level with the masthead, was a small photo of President Assad of Syria. That's the ASSAD who uses chemicals, not to be confused with ASADA, which tries to stop the use of chemicals.

The charge sheet against Essendon and James Hird was very serious, but whatever Hird may or may not have been guilty of doing, whatever compounds and chemicals they may or may not have cooked up for the players, it falls somewhat short of deploying chemical weapons against his own citizens, as Assad is alleged to have done.

Still, as my friend John observed, Hird being banned for 12 months did free him up to take the lead in *Trainspotting 2*.

Coleman watch: One round to go and Roughead (64) leads Travis Cloke of Collingwood by three goals (61) and Jeremy Cameron of GWS by four (60). Go, Rough!

RIDING THE BUMPS ... BUT NOT WITH A GRIN

ROUND 23 – SYDNEY V HAWTHORN
ANZ Stadium, Friday 30 August 2013

It was a sickening feeling. My guts churned for days after this match. Sure, the Hawks had turned on a stirring final-quarter burst for an impressive victory over Sydney in Sydney. And sure, we secured top spot on the ladder, but Buddy's report early in the second quarter for a bump on Nick Malceski prevented me from enjoying any of it.

Just waiting for the verdict left me feeling ill for the entire weekend. It was like having wanton sex with a lascivious beauty only to discover that the condom has broken – you've had the exhilaration but all you're left with is the anxiety.

Not that Malceski didn't deserve a tap after kicking the winning goal in last year's Grand Final, but in a dead rubber (as opposed to a broken one), when in all likelihood we were always going to be playing Sydney again the following week, there was simply no need for any bumping, late or otherwise. Pat him on the back, ask him for beard-grooming tips and get on with the match – that's all that was required. Or, better still, try to smother the ball. Just an idea.

Rarely, you suspect, has a team finishing the home-and-away season on top been left feeling quite so flat leading into the finals. And now we had to play Sydney again, this time without Buddy, who was suspended, while they brought in Kurt Tippett.

There was a school of thought that Hawthorn was better, or at least as good, without Buddy, but I didn't subscribe to such tosh. What team could be improved by removing one of the best players in the competition? It would be like the Stones without Jagger or the Bad Seeds without Nick Cave. They might still play the songs, but not with half the sass and swagger. As a result, I was in a state of deep stress leading into the first final – nothing that wanton sex with a lascivious beauty wouldn't relieve, mind you. I couldn't help feeling that in that one split-second, even if Malceski's jaw wasn't fractured, Hawthorn's premiership campaign might have been.

ROUGH PLAY

On the other hand, we did have the Golden Rough – Jarryd Roughead, our deserving Coleman medallist for 2013!

Rough kicked four goals on Friday night to secure not only the medal but also victory for Hawthorn. His first – and our first, as is often the case – came from a strong mark in front of goal after Buddy spotted him up with a perfectly weighted kick from the centre circle.

His second came in the third quarter: Savage bombed long to the goal square and Rough shot up with an impressive, balletic vertical leap to take the grab. The resulting goal brought us back to within 10 points.

The third came in the final quarter and put us in front. Waiting under a long kick forward, Rough worked his opponent under the ball, which bounced behind them. Rough swung his boot at it indiscriminately, nearly beheading the Poo, who was dashing past to take possession, which he did, then handballed back to Rough, who slid it through to put us in front.

His fourth came barely a minute later, after a ball-up near our goal. Rough took the ball from a Swans tap while simultaneously dislodging a couple of Sydney barnacles and barged through the pack into an open goal. Glorious. Who doesn't love a bit of Rough!

IT'S TIME!

I was watching at home with Oscar in our back room, where he keeps his drum kit. He provided occasional percussive accompaniment to the action while I urged the boys to kick it to Rough.

In truth, the Hawks were outplayed for the first three quarters, trailing by around three goals for the vast majority of the game. And by more than four at one stage in the second quarter. In the language of the election campaign that was raging at the time, we were languishing in the polls. Or, to adopt the ALP's campaign slogan, we needed "a new way" (the ALP marketing team seemingly having forgotten that it was actually they who were in power before the election).

This was the second consecutive week the Hawks had slipped behind by more than four goals. While we had shown impressive fighting qualities to come back and win on both occasions, it was concerning that we were getting into this position in the first place. Put it down to good opponents.

After poor games in the Preliminary and Grand Finals in 2012, Hawthorn people had been at pains to talk about the importance of pacing our performance during 2013 and being primed to peak in September. Well, the finals were starting from the next match, so to quote a more famous and slightly punchier ALP slogan from the past, "It's Time!"

REAL SOLUTIONS. REAL CHANGE.

The game picked up towards the end of the third quarter, with Hawthorn trailing by 21 points. From that moment, Buddy kicked a goal from 50, Savage kicked long for Rough to mark, and Sewell won a hard ball and, got it to Mitchell, who snapped a left-foot goal. Suddenly we were back within four points.

An outrageous decision against Lake gifted Sydney another goal, but after that, Breust wrenched the ball from a pack and handballed to the Poo, who snagged one back for us.

In the final quarter Hawthorn completely dominated, kicking 3.2 to zero in the opening minutes, including a goal to Anderson after a strong tackle was rewarded, and two to Rough. It was truly exhilarating, and my cries of "Rough!" must have echoed across the neighbourhood nearly as loudly as Oscar's ringing cymbal crash when the Hawks hit the front.

In what was hopefully a sign of what we could expect in September, Hodge, Mitchell, Sewell, Lewis, Burgoyne, Roughead and Birchall began to influence every contest. Real leaders providing "real solutions" and "real change", to quote the Liberal Party campaign slogan (in the interests of political balance, of course). These are true leaders standing up for what's important – a Hawthorn win! If we could have been confident that our political aspirants from either side would exert half the doggedness and determination our Hawks showed in the final quarter, the populace might have headed towards the election with a little more enthusiasm.

The game ended on a high, with Breust and Gunston taking marks and kicking accurately to get our lead out beyond three goals. Near the end, like some maverick from the WikiLeaks Party or Palmer United getting in on preferences, even Brian Lake got on the end of a Birchall pass and kicked a long goal to settle the match.

Final scores: Hawthorn 17.10.112 d Sydney Swans 15.4.94
Ladder position: 1st
What we learned: Well, several things, actually: firstly, the brown

back jumper teamed with the brown shorts looks very urban chic, very now. I'm all for this look to continue.

Thanks to Bruce McAvaney, we also found out that no one in the history of the AFL/VFL has ever retired on 322 games. Bruce delivered this bombshell revelation apropos of Jude Bolton's game count up to and including the match against Hawthorn, noting in passing, of course, that as Jude would, in all likelihood, be playing again the following week, then neither would he be retiring on 322 games. It made you wonder how people understood football pre-Bruce.

In previewing the first week of the finals, in which Richmond was set to take on Carlton, Caroline Wilson said on *Footy Classified* that although Richmond had seldom beaten Carlton in recent times (just once in their past 10 meetings) they tend to beat them in finals. And this was true: of their 13 most recent finals, Richmond had won 9, Carlton just 3 and there was one draw.

Of course, the most recent of these matches had been in 2001, when Richmond's current captain, Trent Cotchin, was just 11 years old. The other 12 meetings took place between 1967 and 1982. Of the current playing list, only Chris Newman was actually alive for any of these matches, and even then he was only four months old at the time of the 1982 Grand Final.

I liked Caro's thinking, though. Call me a boring empiricist if you wish, I just thought that matches played between the current groups of players (i.e. the most recent 10 games at the time) might have been a better guide to the likely outcome of the final than matches played between 1967 and 1973, when none of the current players were actually alive.

What we already knew, but didn't want to admit: The game is not what it used to be. Football purists had been mourning this season that the bump was dead and lamenting the loss of this sound defensive strategy. The bump was one thing, but it seemed now that even more enduring and dearly held traditions were under threat from namby-pamby, do-gooder, politically correct modern administrators – I speak, of course, about setting alight dwarves at Mad Monday celebrations.

When St Kilda players set alight a dwarf who had been hired to provide entertainment at their Mad Monday function, most commentators took the view that this was another example of post-season celebrations spiralling out of control. With the notable exception of AFL chief Andrew Demetriou, who, when told of the incident while on Channel 7, simply giggled, possibly recalling similar scenes of overexuberance from his own playing days. It seemed, however, that St Kilda had once again overstepped the bounds of what people find acceptable at this type of function, but once this time-honoured tradition goes the game simply won't be what it was. Just like cricket, which has become so sterile that punching the opposition's opening batsman in a pub ahead of a Test match is now frowned upon. Where did we go so wrong?

HAWTHORN'S MANDATE

It's tempting to draw an analogy between the Coalition's victory in Saturday 7 September's federal election and Hawthorn's victory in the previous night's Qualifying Final. Both were favoured to win and both did so reasonably easily, but while the Coalition victory was clear very early in the contest, Hawthorn's superiority wasn't clear until beyond the halfway mark.

When you check the final scores, however, you see that the Coalition won 90 to 55, whereas Hawthorn's victory was much a more emphatic 105 to 51. That's what I call a mandate.

The Coalition may have been boasting that "It's Tony time" but at Hawthorn we were claiming it as "Hodgey's hour" or "Sammy's stint", for once again they were the stars of the night, along with David Hale and Brad Sewell.

It might also be tempting to find parallels between various individuals from both the Coalition and Hawthorn – for example, compare Tony Abbott's and Luke Hodge's steely resolve, Joe Hockey's and Jarryd Roughead's robust bullocking work, Christopher Pyne's and Jack Gunston's straight shooting (or at least the fact they both come from Adelaide), or Malcolm Turnbull's and Buddy Franklin's vast fortunes. But the analogy falls down when you come to Julie Bishop, for while Clarko might be able to match her death stare, only Dermie can claim to have her hair and her eye for matching accessories, and he's long retired.

I offer no Hawthorn comparison to Barnaby Joyce, for the obvious reason that if such a person existed, we'd have traded him to the Western Bulldogs long ago. Besides, personally I lean to the left politically (unlike the ALP), so comparing my dashing Hawthorn heroes to right-wing neo-conservatives such as Scott Morrison and Greg Hunt (who could take a lesson from Josh Gibson on how to wear glasses without looking like Queen Victoria) leaves me feeling a little queasy.

HUNG PARLIAMENT – THE FIRST HALF

If we're talking politics, though, the first half of Friday night's match resembled the Gillard-led hung parliament: tight, tenacious and tough, with no clear winners and no side holding any real advantage.

Without Buddy and Cyril, it was hard to work out which team held the balance of power. For Hodge, Mitchell and Roughead, Sydney could boast Kieren Jack, Josh Kennedy and Ryan O'Keefe.

There was the occasional highlight, such as Sammy's extraordinary handball out in front of Roughead, who ran on to it and kicked truly from 50, Bradley Hill's run, Matt Spangher's first-quarter goal and commanding presence, but mostly any ground gained was through a scrap – getting the ball forward was a little like Gillard trying to get legislation through both houses.

The two teams going in at half time even on 4.7 apiece reflected how the match had been played. While we might have been lamenting the reduction in our scoring power without Franklin and Rioli, Sydney was finding it tough to score as well. Tippett was proving no real threat as yet, and Gibson, Lake and Guerra were matching them down back.

AHEAD IN THE POLLS – THIRD QUARTER

After the struggle of the first half, the Hawks slowly and methodically edged ahead in the second.

At the end of last season we recruited Brian Lake as a tall, strong defender to help negate players like Kurt Tippett, particularly in the finals (although Lake had played brilliantly all year). And here we were, playing against Tippett after his move from Adelaide to Sydney – a move, if we can allow ourselves to continue the election analogy, that had many football fans demanding of Sydney exactly what the ALP spent the entire campaign demanding of Abbott and Hockey: "Show us your costings!"

Tippett had kicked two first-quarter goals, but Lake had repelled many other opportunities, and early in the third he was running hard forward and doubling back to mark in front of Tippett 50 metres out – from our goal! He then launched into a massive punt, which sailed through post-high! Lake had more than justified his recruitment with this kick alone. And it seemed to break something in Sydney, for a succession of Hawthorn goals ensued.

Some extraordinary running from Isaac Smith (overall it was about five kilometres in the one passage of play) resulted in a pass to Bailey, who marked 25 out from goal and duly converted.

Hodge passed to Hale and Guerra passed to Shiels, resulting in two more set-shot goals. Suddenly we had a four-goal lead. We'd kicked four goals through Lake, Bailey, Hale and Shiels. As a work colleague commented to me post-match, "No Buddy, no Cyril, no worries." The Poo added a nice running goal after some good ruck work from Hale, and we went into the final quarter holding our four-goal advantage.

THE LANDSLIDE VICTORY – THE FINAL QUARTER

We opened the final quarter with Roughead and Anderson both missing set shots. O'Keefe kicked one for the Swans, and our lead was back to 19 points.

But before we had time to get anxious, Roughead stabbed a bullet-like pass to Gunston, who kicked accurately. Further goals to Hale, Roughead and Anderson soon settled the matter and, with it, any nerves.

Anderson's goal came after a brilliant pack mark against two Swans, prompting the gentleman behind me to publicly declare his love for the 19-year-old. The supporter was probably in his late 40s, so I pointed out to him the age difference and the fact that Anderson was already married with a young child. We agreed that these may constitute impediments for some people, but true love, if it's strong enough, will overcome all.

Our affections moved to Breust pretty quickly after he snapped truly to put us 51 points in front. By the end Spangher's every possession, and he was getting a few of them, was greeted with a roar where I was sitting. He was in the side due to Buddy being out suspended and he was playing a strong, competitive role. He was literally obtaining cult status as the match wore on. Jack Gunston continued the goal junket on the siren, and the Hawks had secured power with a decisive 54-point victory.

THE YEAS HAVE IT

It was a great start to the finals campaign, defeating our vanquishers from last season. With Buddy and Cyril to return, we were looking strong just when we needed to.

Final scores: Hawthorn 15.15.105 d Sydney Swans 7.9.51

What we learned: Think local, act global. Just before the match we learnt that Cyril was out with an ankle injury! While this had been widely tipped, my efforts to track down the latest via the Hawthorn app, the AFL app or *The Age* proved fruitless. I finally got the news from Chan-Tha, who was holidaying in New York.

What we already knew: Spangher is the Saviour! Well, he looks like him at least. The idea that Matt Spangher was retaining his place in the team to replace the suspended Buddy Franklin was met with general mirth among most footy fans. It's not that he doesn't try or put in – he certainly does – but it's fair to say he's no Buddy. Which is perhaps unfair in itself, because the same could be said of almost all players in the AFL. Whereas Buddy plays like the messiah, Spangher just looks like him. And as my friend Pete observed, he brings a decent full beard to the team that can better compete with Sydney's bushy miens than the messy stubble that Hodge, the Poo and co. sport.

Freo – friend or foe? In 2012 Fremantle did Hawthorn a favour by knocking Geelong out of the finals, whereas this year they'd knocked them into our path – thanks, Freo. Perhaps we deserved it for not being able to win it in 2012, when they were out of the way.

BLOND HAWTHORN

Thanks to our mighty Qualifying Final win over Sydney, the Hawks had the week off. And it's traditional between weeks one and two of the finals for the AFL to name its All-Australian team – the team that would represent our nation were we to compete in some great international footy tournament.

Of course, on those occasions when we do need to field a national team – to play the hybrid rules game against Ireland – almost none of the All-Australians actually play. Largely because that game is designed for runners, not hulking ruckmen or big defenders, but also because half the players are in a post-operative sling or on a footy trip with their team-mates. So the All-Australian team is largely ornamental, a point which is reinforced when you see who gets selected.

Given that only two Hawthorn players made it in 2013 (Sam Mitchell, on a half-back flank ... seriously? And Jarryd Roughead in a forward pocket ... he won the Coleman Medal so why not full forward?), we're going to boycott it. No Gibbo, who was surely the most outstanding defender of the year, no Buddy, no Hodgey. I figure if the AFL selectors aren't going to take it seriously, why should we?

So my representative team comes without the voice of the AFL (and Tennis Australia and any other sporting body that needs deep, sonorous tones to add authority to their ceremony), Craig Willis, as MC, no official portrait or dinner at Crown, just a can of cheap bleach ... it's the best team of blonds to play for Hawthorn.

Anita Loos's 1925 novel *Gentlemen Prefer Blondes*, later a film starring Marilyn Monroe, may have helped popularise the perhaps spurious notion that blondes are more desirable than brunettes, but something got lost in translation at Hawthorn, where it seems to mean that Gentlemen Prefer Being Blond.

There's something about a bright clear day at the MCG when the sun not only highlights the gold stripes on our jumper and the fans' outfits, but also picks out the highlights in the hair of a Hawthorn on-baller. The Hawks have a long, proud tradition of blonds, possibly only rivalled by St Kilda. From the golden-haired backline of the mid-'70s, via Dermie, Crawf and right through to Mitchell today.

Much is made of the recent recruitment policy of left-footers, but in the mid-'90s, it appeared that blond hair was the basis of our recruitment policy. And if it didn't come naturally, then the players simply shampooed with peroxide. One of the great things about blondness is its inclusivity; anyone can become a blond.

The word "blond" was first known in English in 1481 (14 + 8 + 1 = 23 ... spooky) and derives from the Old French word "blund" or "blont", meaning "a colour midway between golden and light chestnut" – in other words, a colour between brown and gold ... a Hawthorn colour.

The colour itself is characterised by low levels of the dark pigment eumelanin, and while there are different blond hues – platinum, sandy, strawberry et cetera – the predominant characteristic is a variant of yellow, and it sits on the colour wheel between yellow and light brown. What to conclude other than it's a Hawthorn hue.

And here's the best team of Hawthorn blonds:

Back: Brian Douge, Ryan Schoenmakers, Andy Collins

Half Back: Ian Bremner, Peter Knights, Bohdan Jaworski

Centre: Chris Wittman, Sam Mitchell, Russell Morris

Half Forward: Peter Curran, Dermott Brereton, Paul Hudson

Forward: Michael Osborne, Gary Ablett Sr, Daniel Chick

Followers: Richard Walter, Peter Crimmins (captain), Shane Crawford (vice captain)

Interchange from: Kevin Ablett, Rick Ladson, Rayden Tallis, Michael McCarthy, Simon Crawshay, Matthew Robran, Justin Crawford, Paul Barnard, Will Langford (just in case he turns out to be as good as his father)

Coach: Allan Jeans

PETER CRIMMINS – CAPTAIN OF THE BLONDS

Crimmo might have begun it all – those of us who saw him play will instantly picture his little blond bob bouncing up and down as he ran after the ball. There may have been Hawthorn blonds before him, but he set the new template. Surely giving Sam Mitchell Crimmo's famous number 5 was based as much on Mitchell's hair as it was on his style of play.

Crimmo is joined on the ball by Crawford, an obvious choice, and Richard Walter, who gets first ruck ahead of Crawshay, though Crawshay was much funnier to watch, and one of our forgotten great number 23s. Not our best blond 23, of course; that mantle can only be bestowed on Dermie.

Dermie is the centrepoint of the half-forward line and arguably sported the greatest permed blond mullet known to human history. As with our best exports team and our 1991 Grand Final team, again he edges out Matthew Robran for the centre half-forward position. Dermie is joined on the half-forward line by Peter Curran and son of

Huddo, Paul Hudson. Both great and both blond, even if Huddo's wasn't entirely natural.

Gary Ablett Sr leads our forward line. Sure, he didn't play many games for Hawthorn, but he did play some and he did have blond, if wispy, hair. Just enough of both to qualify. And as it turned out, he was a pretty good full forward too. So he's an obvious pick.

Daniel "Chicky Babe" Chick and "Radar" Tallis epitomise the surfie blond look of the mid-'90s and are included as a nod to a great blond era.

Peter Knights is one of the great Hawthorn blonds, possibly the greatest "natural" blond player of all time: natural in talent and hue. He formed the centrepoint of the great blond backline of the '70s with Brian Douge, Ian Bremner, Bohdan Jaworski and Alle de Wolde (who was sort of blond) – most of whom made it into the team above.

Andy Collins is an obvious addition from our great '80 to '90s line-up and Ryan "The Cobbler" Schoenmakers gets in because we needed a tall, blond backman.

It's a formidable line-up and one, I suspect, that would not only defeat the All-Australian team in a football match, but would look a whole lot more convincing at the beach.

WAIT LONG BY THE RIVER AND THE BODIES OF YOUR ENEMIES WILL FLOAT BY

PRELIMINARY FINAL – HAWTHORN V GEELONG
MCG, Friday 20 September 2013

Wait Long By the River and the Bodies of Your Enemies Will Float By is the title of the second album by The Drones. It is reportedly an ancient Japanese proverb, but might just be a made-up maxim attributed to the Japanese by Sean Connery in the 1993 movie *Rising Sun*. Whatever the origin of the saying, its central message of "Good things come to those who wait" or "Patience is a virtue" or "Up yours, Geelong!" has most Hawks fans nodding in recognition.

In fact, Hawks fans taking the trek from the G to the city after the Preliminary Final might have taken a glance at the lapping brown tide of the Yarra and been able to make out in the murk the slime-coated, litter-bedecked empty vessels of our long-time adversaries Steve Johnson and Joel Selwood, Jimmy Bartel, Tom Lonergan, Joel Corey, James Kelly and Andrew Mackie all drifting quietly past. Bon voyage, boys …

JEFF WAS RIGHT!

In the lead-up to the match there was, as always when these sides meet, much talk about the Kennett curse. On the eve of the 2009 season, after defeating Geelong in the 2008 Grand Final, Hawthorn president Jeff Kennett said that Geelong didn't have the mental toughness to defeat Hawthorn in big games.

"They don't have the psychological drive we have. We've beaten Geelong when it matters," is what he actually said.

As we all know, the Hawks hadn't beaten the Cats in their 11 subsequent meetings, giving rise to the notion of the curse.

Now, having now finally defeated Geelong, much was being made of the fact that the curse was now broken. But was there ever really a curse? And really, didn't Friday night's events prove that Jeff was right, after all?

If you examine his exact quote, you'll see he was referring to "when it matters". He said nothing about the piddling home-and-away games that make up 10 of the 11 losses. And the other was a Qualifying Final, not a knock-out, do-or-die encounter. So of the last five games that really "mattered", Hawthorn had won every one of them: 1989 Grand Final, 1991 Second Semi Final, 2000 Elimination Final, 2008 Grand Final and 2013 Preliminary Final. (I wasn't alive when the 1963 Grand Final was played, so I'm not including that. Although interestingly, I would have been conceived at around about that time, but let's not follow that thread.)

Geelong fans can do their gloating over home-and-away games if they like (and, as any Hawthorn fan knows, they haven't held back), but we'll save ours for the matches that matter.

MISSING THE TARGET

Of course, anyone watching the match would have been forgiven for thinking the curse was still active, for surely some malevolent supernatural entity or evil spirit was putting a hex on our set shots for goal.

In no particular order, Hale (twice), Breust (thrice), Lewis, Shiels,

Roughead and Gunston all missed relatively straightforward set shots for goal. There may well have been others, but by the final quarter I was no longer able to watch when we were lining up. I just waited for the collective moan to tell the story before I lifted my head.

They were spraying it everywhere, like men aiming into a toilet bowl after 11 pm at a party. Honestly, you'd think the goal face was a narrow aperture in the space–time continuum that appeared only fleetingly like a slim, wavering tear, just long enough for Dr Who to slip through in the Tardis, before quickly closing up. As Matthew (19:24) sayeth, quoting Jesus, "Again I tell you, it is easier for a camel to go through the eye of a needle than for the Hawks to slot one through the big sticks at the G."

MORE EBB THAN FLOW

The match began inauspiciously, and I don't mean the free kick the umpire paid to Geelong within seconds of the start, but the woman behind me, who'd grabbed my shoulder to pull me down after I stood to cheer on the Hawks during a stoppage. Then when I turned to enquire if she thought she was at the ballet, her husband pulled my cap over my eyes. I think they thought it was the 1989 Grand Final and they were actually playing for Geelong. On half time when I cheered Rough's big mark, I overheard their daughter suggesting that her dad jab me in the ribs! In retrospect, I'm lucky they didn't take me out at the first bounce, Mark Yeates style. They must be accustomed to watching footy down at Simonds Stadium, where they never have to encounter opposition supporters. The worst part was I hadn't even begun to be obnoxious.

For two and a half quarters Hawthorn had the ascendency in general play but we were simply unable to convert our opportunities. Whereas when Geelong went forward they rarely missed. Steve

Johnson was playing a brilliant game for Geelong and looked set to decide the course of the match on his own, Jimmy Bartel was playing well as always and being generally handsome, and they were easily covering the loss of our arch-nemesis Paul Chapman.

Both teams enjoyed periods of superiority. Geelong got out to a 19-point lead in the second quarter before Hawthorn clawed back and edged in front, point by agonising point. Our inaccuracy was becoming a crucial factor, in particular Roughead's miss after the half-time siren. After taking a soaring mark on the edge of the goal square, he managed to miss the goal, somewhat sapping the momentum we'd been building.

The third quarter opened fairly evenly, but when Birchall ran through Mathew Stokes it resulted in a Jimmy Bartel goal, a scuffle and a short but decisive period when the hex kicked in and everything went wrong for Hawthorn and right for Geelong.

Joel Selwood and Cameron Guthrie kicked goals, then, after Burgoyne got one back for us, Cyril took an absolute screamer in the goal square, but either it wasn't paid or he decided playing on in the goal square while sitting down was a good percentage play – or, more likely, it was an earthly manifestation that there is no God. Either way, it resulted in Geelong sweeping the ball forward and Steven Motlop kicking a goal. Harry Taylor kicked another over his shoulder. Then, with the ball bobbling near the boundary, it came off a Geelong boot, as the replay clearly illustrated, but the sheer force of Geelong whingeing left the umpires undecided – even though everyone at the ground and everyone watching on TV could tell exactly what happened – and they elected to ball it in, from which, of course, Geelong scored again.

In the space of five minutes and two or three crucial moments where baffling calls had gone against us, our one-point deficit had blown out to a 20-point deficit at three-quarter time. I was not alone among Hawthorn fans in thinking we were gone.

THREE-QUARTER-TIME SULKING

Taking stock at three-quarter time: Sam Mitchell was playing one of his best ever games – which is saying something; Hale and Burgoyne were playing well; but Franklin, Roughead, Hodge and Sewell were all well below their normal standard and having very little impact. We were 20 points down, and a season that had progressed quite swimmingly seemed destined to end in an all too predictable fashion.

I've been to every Grand Final since 1971 except for two: in 1996 I was overseas, and in 1999 I was at home with a newborn. As the Hawks broke from their huddle, however, I decided that I simply couldn't bear to attend the Grand Final this year if Hawthorn wasn't playing. After being the dominant side all year, to not even make the Grand Final seemed just too depressing a scenario to face.

I was in full sulk mode, and that newborn from 1999 was sitting next to me at the game feeling exactly the same. As was Chan-Tha, who, having returned from her holiday, was wishing she was back in Jamaica.

FROM GRIEF TO BELIEF

When Franklin got his boot on the end of a loose ball in the goal square I thought we had a slight chance. The field umpire signalled "all clear", the goal umpire stuck out his two fingers and did his little semaphore thing with the flags and everyone went back to position. Then someone sitting in a sort of panic room somewhere decided that the goal needed to be reviewed. So ignoring the fact that two umpires were standing close by and 36 players had settled on a decision, they decided they'd like to intervene and slow things up. I wasn't even aware there was allowance for this sort of thing in the rules, and I can't help feeling that, had it been anyone other than Buddy whose toe had nudged the ball through, play would simply have resumed.

If two blokes watching on TV can just stop the game at any given moment, why didn't they intervene when Cyril's mark wasn't paid? Why didn't they intervene when Geelong kicked the ball out on the full and the umpires called for a ball-in? You can tell I was becoming agitated.

After Josh Caddy kicked one for Geelong it was back to 19 points and it stayed that way for several crucial minutes. It was 96 to 77 at the 13-minute mark, and I recalled Leigh Matthews's elegantly simple theory that the first team to 100 usually wins. At that moment it didn't look like it could possibly be Hawthorn. We still trailed by more than three goals and I'd moved beyond fearing the worst and was well into the second or third stage of the grief cycle.

BURGOYNE BRINGS IT HOME

Then it turned. The Hawks were getting on top all over the ground. Gibson and Stratton down back. Mitchell and Hodge in the middle, and up front, Gunston and Burgoyne. It was Shaun Burgoyne who pretty much decided he wasn't going to let the Hawks lose. His tackle on Jimmy Bartel caused the Geelong champ's attempted clearing kick to drop short, where it landed with Bradley Hill, who ran in and goaled.

Then Burgoyne, tracking back, retrieved the ball and showed poise to handball it to Gunston for another.

And then, after tackling Mackie, Burgoyne was on the end of a chain of handballs from Lewis and Gunston and ran in himself to put us in front! The vision of him running off in celebration with his arms outstretched as if he was hugging the world would become the defining image of the finals.

Of course, there were several behinds littered among this burst and several more to come, but we found ourselves in an eerily familiar position – six points up with, well, who knew how long left.

As the Hawks clung on to the lead, we clung on to one another in our seats. This would rate as five or so of the most nerve-wracking minutes I've ever experienced at the football. But strangely, all those close losses to Geelong since 2008 somehow steeled me. I was expecting the worst, and I knew what that looked like, but it wasn't happening. Hawthorn seemed to be holding on strongly and it was Geelong players who were mishandling the ball.

Ben Stratton took two big pack marks from Geelong kick-ins, Burgoyne was in everything, Cyril was just starting to get involved, Mitchell simply didn't let the ball get past him, and suddenly we believed ... until Geelong broke free one last time and got the ball to Travis Varcoe, who was in space about 30 metres out ... But before we even had time to form the thought 'My God, it's happening again, I can't believe it', Varcoe missed! For once Geelong had missed!

As Hawthorn brought the ball around the outer wing, the noise was such that no one heard the final siren when it rang. Cyril had it 15 metres out and he played on to Buddy, which therefore didn't count. But it didn't matter. We'd won! We'd beaten Geelong! More importantly, we'd made it to the Grand Final!

"What just happened?" read the text from my Hawthorn friend Linda, who was somewhere in the ground.

GOAL DANCING

A misguided decision to drive to the game meant that I couldn't celebrate in a manner befitting the occasion – guzzling champagne, lubing up and climbing nude up one of the goal posts while waving a Hawthorn flag. That was something that could wait for when we won the Grand Final. YOLO.

Defeating Geelong by less than a goal in a final was a fitting way to end the hoodoo. On the one hand, it would have been nice to bury them, as our shots on goal suggested we should have, but that would have given the Geelong players and fans time to get accustomed to the idea of losing, to frame it in a philosophical light, and even leave early. Whereas this way they got to experience a little of what Hawks fans have felt over the past 11 meetings as we'd been overrun in the final quarter or lost on the final kick. Except on this occasion there was a Grand Final appearance at stake.

My thoughts turned to the Geelong fan sitting in front of me in Round 1 who had actually wished death upon Buddy; to all those Cats fans I know who have Facebooked and texted me after Geelong has beaten us in the past five years; and to the people behind me at this match who, naturally, had left before I had a chance to wish them a pleasant drive back to South Barwon. In fact, they'd left before we reached "We love our club!" in the first rendition of the song. So since they couldn't stay, I applauded the Geelong players off on their behalf. After all, they'd played a great match and had a wonderful season. They were just beaten by a team whose destiny was to win the 2013 premiership.

Final scores: Hawthorn 14.18.102 d Geelong 15.7.97

What we learned: All hoodoos end, all curses are broken. In the earlier chapter about the Geelong v Hawthorn Groundhog Day experience in Round 15, I lamented that a Brit (even though he's actually a Scot) had managed to win Wimbledon while Hawthorn still couldn't defeat Geelong. There I was thinking this was a sign that the hoodoo might last forever, when in fact it was telling me that all hoodoos end. I mean, even Geelong won a premiership in 2007 after 44 years and five Grand Final losses.

Spain eventually won a World Cup in 2010 after 80 years, England reclaimed the Ashes in 2005 after 16 years, Adam

Scott became the first Australian to win the US Masters in 2013 after several close calls by his countrymen, and Australia won the America's Cup in 1983 after 129 years.

Even if it did exist, the Kennett curse is mild by comparison to some others. In rugby Ireland has never beaten the All Blacks, and the Welsh haven't beaten them since 1953.

The most famous sporting curse is "The curse of the Bambino" in baseball. In 1918, after winning the World Series, the Boston Red Sox sold Babe Ruth to the New York Yankees. In footy terms, it was a bit like letting Gary Ablett Sr go to Geelong. Like Ablett, Babe Ruth furthered his reputation with the Yankees, but the difference is that while Hawthorn won their way to seven successive Grand Finals and eight of the next nine without Ablett, winning five of them, the Red Sox endured an 86-year drought, until they finally ended it in 2004.

Melbourne is suffering under a similar curse. After legendary coach Norm Smith took them to the 1964 premiership, his sixth overall as coach of Melbourne, they sacked him during the 1965 season, and they haven't won since.

My favourite sporting curse, however, involves the Socceroos and a witch doctor. I mean, if a curse is to be taken seriously there should be a witch doctor involved, not just a former state premier. Of course, many on the left of politics might place Jeff Kennett in that category anyway.

The story was first related in Johnny Warren's autobiography, *Sheilas, Wogs and Poofters*. The Australian team was playing Rhodesia (now Zimbabwe) in 1969 in Mozambique and was trying to qualify for the 1970 World Cup. They organised for a witch doctor to place a curse on Rhodesia, which he did by burying some bones near the goal posts and presumably chanting some incantations and moving his body in dance.

Australia won the match 3–1, but when the witch doctor asked for payment, the team couldn't provide it. So the witch doctor reversed the curse and placed it on Australia.

Australia did qualify for the 1974 World Cup, but were drawn to play host Germany and were duly thumped. Since then they had never qualified again, despite being 2–0 up against Iran in the second half at the MCG in 1997, needing only to hang on to win, and in 2001 losing to Uruguay in the final qualifier.

The curse was eventually lifted by comedian and writer John Safran in his show *John Safran versus God*. He travelled to Mozambique to find the witch doctor and have him reverse the curse.

As it happened, the witch doctor had died, but Safran found another witch doctor who could channel the original one. Safran explained in an interview with *The Age* on 20 November 2005 that he and the witch doctor had to sit in the centre of the pitch while the witch doctor slaughtered a chicken and covered Safran in its blood.

John Safran then went to Telstra Stadium with Johnny Warren and they washed themselves in clay that the witch doctor had provided. At the next qualifying stage for the 2006 World Cup, Australia defeated Uruguay and got through.

Okay, I think everyone would like to see Jeff Kennett covered in chicken's blood in the middle of the MCG, but, failing that, defeating Geelong by less than a goal will just have to do.

Now we just had to give Freo the old heave-ho.

What we already knew: That with Paul Chapman out suspended, it was our best chance yet of defeating Geelong since 2008. It may be apocryphal but Chapman had vowed after the 2008

Grand Final that Geelong would never lose to Hawthorn again. And he upheld his side of the bargain, or "Cat pact" as it's become known, combining with Bartel to get us every time.

By 2014 Chapman was a restricted free agent and joined Essendon. I advocated that Hawthorn should recruit him, not to play, as such, but just to make sure he never plays against us.

Addendum: The very next day the Box Hill Hawks defeated Geelong in the VFL Grand Final. In an eerie echo of the 2008 AFL season, Geelong had won 13 games in succession leading into the match and was strong favourite to go back-to-back. But in a stunning upset, the mighty Hawks kicked away early and stayed in front for the entire match.

PARADISE REGAINED –
THE HAWTHORN ZEITGEIST
Hawthorn ... Premiers 2013!

GRAND FINAL – HAWTHORN V FREMANTLE
MCG, Saturday 28 September 2013, attendance 100,007

In the first chapter of this epic tale, we looked at Milton's poem "Paradise Lost" and saw parallels between the fall of man and the fall of Hawthorn in the 2012 decider. Moving on to the sequel, "Paradise Regained", we saw that it could be read as an allegory for how the 2013 season would unfold – where what was lost in 2012 would be regained in 2013 – and that is exactly what had come to pass.

Paradise regained indeed. We are the zeitgeist!

... a fiery Globe
Of Angels on full sail of wing flew nigh
Who on their plumy Vans receiv'd him soft
From his uneasie station, and upbore
As on a floating couch through the blithe Air,
Then in a flowry valley set him down
On a green bank, and set before him spred
A table of Celestial Food, Divine
Ambrosial, Fruits fetcht from the tree of life

And from the fount of life Ambrosial drink,
That soon refresh'd him wearied, and repair'd
What hunger, if aught hunger had impair'd
Or thirst, and as he fed, Angelic Quires
Sung Heavenly Anthems of his victory ...

Okay, so it's a little more baroque than Mark "Robbo" Robinson of the *Herald-Sun* might put it, but it's a fairly clear description of Luke Hodge being chaired around the ground on the lap of honour, taken back to the rooms and there refreshed with ambrosial water from the Fount of Life – or the premiership cup, as we know it.

The angelic choirs singing "heavenly anthems of victory" is a clear reference to the mighty swarm of Hawks fans belting out the team song at the ground, as well as the players' rendition in the winners' circle in the rooms.

It was a great triumph. A tour de force!

Yes, I cried, I fist-pumped and high-fived. I hugged strangers and sang out loud and out of tune, but what a glorious day ...

Let's go back to the beginning of the week and track the final chapter of Hawthorn's 11th premiership as it took shape.

GRAND FINAL WEEK DIARY
Sunday 22 September 2013

We know our opponent – it's Hawthorn v Fremantle. Fremantle played impressively well to defeat Sydney the previous night, exerting intense pressure on the Swans and, with a rabid crowd behind them, they've got people talking.

So much so that Channel 9's *Sunday Footy Show* panel all pick Freo to win the big one. Ryan Crowley is suddenly cast as the potential match winner, Hayden Ballantyne as the most dangerous key forward on the day. It's seemingly been forgotten that the Hawks have won 21 of 24 games so far and achieved key wins – Sydney in Round 7 and Essendon in Round 18 – through intense tackling pressure. And that in our only encounter with Fremantle, the Hawks enjoyed an untroubled 42-point win. Surely, reason will prevail by the end of the week.

Monday 23 September 2013 – Brownlow night

Another baffling night at the Brownlow when not one of Hawthorn's good and great wins the award. It seems the umpires don't think much of us either. On seven occasions when Hawthorn won the match, a player from the opposition was awarded the three votes. Okay, one of them was Gary Ablett, so fair enough, but six others, including Josh Kennedy from the Eagles in Round 13 – seriously?

Despite winning 19 games, more than any other team, we only came fourth on the vote tally – a full 12 votes behind leader Sydney. I can't be sure, but I think that maybe under AFL rules Sydney receives extra Brownlow votes as part of their salary cap. It's part of their living-outside-the-rules allowance.

While I'm disappointed Sam Mitchell didn't win, I didn't really think he would. He'd been hanging about at half back for large parts of the year, and the ball wasn't down there all that much. But really, had anyone other than Ablett won it, the award would have had to have been abandoned due to a lack of relevance, like the NAB Cup or the Gold Logie.

Tuesday 24 September 2013 – Go west

Former *Herald-Sun* footy journalist and Fox Footy host Mike Sheahan posits his belief that, win or lose, Alastair Clarkson will leave Hawthorn and coach West Coast next season. What a bizarre story to run with in Grand Final week. Even worse, all football journalists picked up the errant ball and ran with it.

It was as ludicrous as the Canberra press gallery trying to bring on a government leadership spill in the lead-up to the election ... oh wait, they did. Unlike the Rudd–Gillard stand-off, however, there seems to be no basis whatsoever for this assertion that could have no outcome other than to create an unnecessary distraction to Hawthorn's preparation.

Mike, of course, is famous for his, in my view, meaningless Top 50 player lists. Were we to draw up such a list for footy journalists, and I adopt the broadest possible definition of the term, we'd have to position him somewhere below Mark "Malcontent" Maclure and Patrick "Moral Guardian of the Game" Smith, perhaps just above Robbo.

Over on *Footy Classified* and *Talking Footy,* they're also going for Freo. I mean, it didn't surprise me that Matthew Lloyd picked them, but even Garry Lyon, who is one of the sharpest observers of the game and someone you can usually rely on to see through the hype, is going for Freo. Ryan Crowley is assuming Ablett-like powers since his last game. This is just weird.

Thursday 26 September 2013 – The Footy Show

The Footy Show is as much a part of Grand Final week as an office handball competition, but even less likely to hit the bull's eye. I turned over to *Would I Lie to You?* on the ABC, wondering if perhaps it's another show in which Mike Sheahan makes bold predictions for 2014, but no, it's an English panel show. Funnier, of course, than *The Footy Show,* with the added advantage of not featuring a player revue, a cringe-worthy, overblown high-school karaoke night with a huge wardrobe budget.

The majority of panellists on *The Footy Show* also go for Freo (Jonathan Brown being an exception) and the Purple Haze is being talked up. After all, they've beaten Geelong and Sydney! (The panel having seemingly forgotten that Hawthorn did as well.)

Ryan Crowley by now is better than Gary Ablett Sr and Jr combined. I'm beginning to wonder how Freo has lost any matches at all with him in their ranks. I go back and watch the Round 4 clash from Aurora – Ballantyne does nothing special, Crowley barely gets a touch. Hold on, I lie; Crowley did miss a goal from 20 centimetres out – hard to do, really. He must be good. Yet in the Grand Final-week commentary they loom larger than Chris Judd and Michael Voss, to say nothing of Hodge, Mitchell, Franklin, Roughead et al., who everyone seems to have forgotten will also be playing.

I think it's a case of the commentariat simply jumping on board with the last thing they saw, which in this case was Fremantle.

History may not necessarily repeat, but you can sometimes draw comfort from it. I recall 1983 and 1988, when Essendon and Melbourne respectively won their way through to play Hawthorn in the Grand Final. Neither had been to the Grand Final for many years, and both had powered though the finals from the Elimination. By Grand Final week, everyone had forgotten Hawthorn was even in it – let alone that we'd got there first by being consistently better all season. We duly defeated them by 83 and 96 points respectively. I await a similar result on Saturday.

The theory gaining most traction in the media was that Hawthorn had lost the previous Grand Final to Sydney, which had finished third. And this year Freo had also finished third. As patterns go, it was fairly rudimentary, at least as a barometer for predicting the future. I preferred to reflect on the fact that when the other WA team, the West Coast Eagles, made it to their first Grand Final in 1991, they also came up against Hawthorn. We thrashed them, and I suspected there'd be a repeat with Fremantle.

Friday 27 September 2013 – the Grand Final parade

The kids join me at work and we wander up to the top of Spring Street for the parade. The Freo fans have turned the town purple as the week has worn on and they are out in force again today, droning their monotonous and annoying "Freeeooh … Freeeooh" chant. They seem unusually brash and confident for supporters of a team that's never made it before, and has only just brushed off its "laughing stock" reputation.

Perhaps they're just excited to be here, and why not? We are. Or they're trying to justify the thousands of dollars they had to spend to get here. After all, it could be a long trip home via Singapore, which is how many of them have travelled. Hopefully they can pick up some good duty-free bargains to make it worth their while. Hawks fans, on the other hand, just seem happy to be enjoying some rare Melbourne sunshine.

The Hawks boys look relaxed and ready. Buddy and Gibbo are among the last to chug up the hill – perhaps they stopped off at a couple of boutiques on the way up Collins Street to pick up some accessories. They also seem to have acquired some children along the way – acquired or sired, one or the other.

Friday night it's Grand Final Eve drinks with Chan-Tha. We go to Cabinet, an upstairs bar with a laneway entry, hidden enough that the ubiquitous Freo fans won't find it.

Saturday 28 September 2013 – Grand Final Day dawns

I mean that literally. As an MCC member I had to queue, having missed out on the reserved-seat ballot, so I was there well before dawn. I arrived in Yarra Park at around 2.45 am, around 12 hours to the bounce, and was one of several hundred shadowy figures lurking between the trees.

Queuing before dawn at the G is one of the curious rites of spring in Melbourne. There's a sense of restlessness as people uncork thermoses (or, in the case of the fellas behind me, snap open cans of Jim Beam) and whisper in hushed tones, settle under makeshift canopies or doze uneasily on camp chairs while they wait for dawn. It's dark so you can't make out features. Even those whose faces are illuminated by the mini-stage lighting of iPads and Kindles are hidden beneath beanies, scarves and balaclavas.

I was without a chair but lucked in when the bloke behind me took his car back home and left me his seat for a few hours. Happily, there was no rain, but around 4 am the cold kicked in just as the earth turned towards dawn.

The MCC offers coffee – it's instant and the water lukewarm, but the task of getting it is at least a distraction. As the light lifts you can make out the faces of the people you've been talking to. I'm reassured that other Hawthorn fans are equally baffled by the surge in support for Fremantle.

By 7 am, one hour before the gates open, there's the bustle of movement as people fold tarps and rugs, dismantle tents and gather cushions and pillows to return them to cars. There's a sense of an army getting ready for battle, a sense heightened when the makeshift borders are taken down and we begin to shuffle forward, and I hear the cry of "once more over the breach!"

The queue is 15 across and stretches right back to the top of the gardens and around the corner. I'm near the front and see Craig Hutchison taking a photo of the queue he doesn't have to join. There's one Fremantle fan in the queue who has been interviewed by at least three different TV stations – he'll have his own show by the time the match starts.

Finally the gates open at 8 am and I secure a fantastic spot in the front row on level two of the MCC Members' stand. I'll have an unimpeded panoramic view of everything; that's assuming I can stay awake.

Once you've got your seat ticket you can leave, so I meet my brother Graeme for our now traditional Grand Final breakfast at Il Solito Posto in a laneway off Collins Street. The owner is pleased to see some brown and gold in the room and our order for beers at 11 am is greeted with cheers from the kitchen – the first beers of the day. At last, these cheers say, real footy fans. Grand Final Day is here ...

THE RITE OF SPRING

The Grand Final is colloquially known as the "Big Dance". It's unclear why, but perhaps because, like the high-school social, there's the prospect of "picking up" at the end of it. Particularly if you're on the winning team. Whatever the origin of the saying, we were certainly hoping to see Cyril and Buddy bust some moves.

In 2013 the reference to the Big Dance perhaps has more resonance because it is the 100th anniversary of the first performance of *The Rite of Spring*, the famous ballet by Igor Stravinsky and Vaslav Nijinsky. *The Rite of Spring* celebrates in music and dance the pagan rituals of spring, which in Melbourne in September can only mean the Grand Final.

In the ballet the performers embark on a series of dances that symbolise them becoming one with the earth and giving thanks for its bounty. There is a dance called the "Ritual of the Rival Tribes", which carries a clear Grand Final theme of the opposing fans coming together. This dance is followed by the "Procession of the Sage", during which Hawthorn takes the field.

In the second half there is a dance called "Mystic Circles of the Young Girls", which is presumably set later in the night. We'll move on. In "Evocation of the Ancestors", ageing Hawthorn fans like me dance out tales about the glory days of the '80s – that bit goes for a while – while "Glorification of the Chosen One" sees Brian Lake take centre stage for a dynamic solo.

The ballet concludes with the "Sacrificial Dance", in which the chosen girl dances herself to death as a sacrifice to the pagan gods, a clear symbol of the exertion, endeavour and determination the Hawks displayed, their preparedness to "pay the price", as Allan Jeans might have had it.

The opening performance of *The Rite of Spring* in 1913 was greeted with a hostile reception from the audience – heckling, jeering, booing – not unlike the reception Hawthorn fans were able to give Crowley and Ballantyne after their debut Grand Final performance.

Of course, *The Rite of Spring* is most famous for the music. Now a staple of the classical repertoire, it is synonymous with bold invention and wild experimentation, much like Clarko's game plan or Cyril paddling the ball through a pack.

However, if we were to tell the story of the Grand Final in song, there's only one song that can really encapsulate the day, and that is, of course, the Hawthorn theme song. Cue the trad-jazz quartet, the banjo player and get ready for the trumpet solo.

We're a happy team at Hawthorn

Well, "happy" isn't the word – more like delirious. I wept, I quaffed Veuve Clicquot, I hugged grown men I've never met before, and that was without even activating my Grindr app.

We're the mighty fighting Hawks

The game was tough and rugged, and this was no more exemplified than after five minutes when it was five tackles to zero (our way). And after Mitchell went down twice in the first quarter, Buddy put Crowley down, once illegally, for which he was penalised, but on another occasion he hip-and-shouldered Crowley as he took possession and sent him sprawling. Cyril laid several crunching tackles, and in one memorable passage Hawthorn just muscled the ball forward without taking possession, until eventually winning a free kick.

Despite what the pundits thought, Hawthorn's tackling was fiercer and stronger and we were exerting such pressure that Freo simply wasn't getting any clean disposals and were duffing those they did.

We love our club

I love Hawthorn more than ever after Saturday's win. And it's a love that borders on the irrational, perhaps even the unnatural, and quite possibly the illegal in some states, but it's love nonetheless.

As I pointed out in an earlier chapter, most football fans are more likely to be unfaithful to their partners than to their football teams. Regardless of my marital status, I'd welcome it if Rihanna wanted to push me to the ground and strut up and down my spine in her heels, but I could never support any team other than Hawthorn.

And we play to win

This is really where Hawthorn differentiates itself from Fremantle, because we try to win by moving the ball forwards and kicking goals. Simple, really. It's less clear how Fremantle hopes to win big games with all their players packed into the opposition's 50-metre arc. Brian Lake was able to take mark after mark, particularly in the final quarter, as there were no Freo players up forward to stop him.

Preventing the opposition from scoring is indeed part of the puzzle, and Fremantle excels in this, but at some point you have to try to score yourself, and that seems to be the bit they haven't quite figured out yet.

Fremantle coach Ross Lyon has now had teams in four Grand Finals (including three times with St Kilda) and the biggest tally of goals any of them have kicked is 10. You don't win many fans with such a game plan, but you're even less likely to win a Grand Final with 10 goals.

Riding the bumps with a grin, at Hawthorn

Riding the bumps, alright – Mitchell took plenty, Buddy running back into an oncoming Chris Mayne was inspirational – the match was full of heroic acts. When I hear this line of the song, I think not only of the hits and bumps we absorbed in the Grand Final, and there were plenty, but of Brendan Whitecross. Two years in succession he's injured his knee in the finals and missed the Grand Final, yet he has only ever shown a relaxed and philosophical, even positive, outlook.

When the siren went on Saturday he was one of the first out on the ground (well, perhaps not the first, given that he was on crutches) to hug his replacement, Jonathan Simpkin.

Of course, he might do well to change his name from a well-known instrument of sacrifice to something less tempting to fate – something warmer and more nurturing, like Whitekitten or Whitewomb.

Come what may, you'll find us striving

In the third quarter, when Fremantle were charging at us and getting on top, the Hawks kept going and bustled their way back into it. It was claustrophobic and stifling in the packs, but the Hawks held on and scored key goals at crucial moments – none more so than when Hill got it to Gunston, who snapped from the goal square to put us 10 points in front.

Shiels and Gibbo collided while trying to spoil, but Birchall was there, leaping over a prone Shiels as he gathered the ball, firing off a handball that started a chain to Stratton, back to Gibbo, over to Lewis and then to Hale just as the siren sounded. No score but still striving.

It's not a battle unless there's a chance the result could go either way, and the third quarter proved to be pivotal. Hawthorn absorbed Freo's best shots and then fired their own. In "Paradise Regained" Christ triumphs over Satan, but the tale has no moral substance unless there was a chance he might not. Come what may ...

Teamwork is the thing that talks ... four, three, two

In the second quarter, Mitchell tackled Crowley to dispossess him. Buddy charged forward to grab the ball, handballed immediately to an oncoming Cyril, who passed to Gunston to run in and kick a long goal from 50. Teamwork that talks ...

Not long after this incident, Ballantyne marked 35 metres out. He could have passed quickly to Walters, who had cruised into the goal square by himself, but decided to take the kick himself ... which he duly duffed. Teamwork that isn't on speaking terms ...

That was the difference – the Hawks worked with and for one another all day. Fremantle's much vaunted defence was beaten by Hawthorn's even better defence. Lake, Gibson, Stratton, Guerra, Hodge and Birchall combined beautifully all day. Hence why Fremantle went in at half time with an embarrassing scoreline of 1.6.12.

One for all and all for one is the way we play at Hawthorn

Much has been made of Mitchell being held by Crowley, and while he may not have won as many possessions as usual, he was in everything. In the final quarter, in quick succession he upended both Nathan Fyfe and Michael Johnson as they were each about to shoot towards goal. No possessions, but two match-saving acts.

The Poo didn't have many clean possessions, but in the final quarter he fought and fought to keep the ball in our forward pocket, holding off three Fremantle defenders in a gang tackle. Moments later he kicked the ball forward for Hill to run on to it and kick the sealer.

As the statistics show, Hawthorn had a very even spread of possession winners across the team, showing that this was a collective effort. Lake and Gunston stood out at either end, but only because of the hard work from those in between.

We are the mighty fighting Hawks!

We are indeed mighty – a team that has been handcrafted to meet our own unique needs. Burgoyne, Guerra, Gibson, Gunston, Hale, Simpkin and Lake – all brought in from other clubs to play particular roles. In the argot of today, Hawthorn is truly a bespoke team.

Hawthorn's fighting spirit came to the fore throughout the latter stages of the season. Against North Melbourne in Round 22, Sydney in Round 23 and Geelong in the Preliminary Final, the team trailed either late in the third quarter or into the final quarter, yet in each match fought to keep in touch and fought further to get ahead and win. Even in the Grand Final, although we were ahead for the entire match, Fremantle challenged in the third quarter and Hawthorn had to fight to maintain the ascendancy.

Hawthorn's complete dominance early in the final quarter,

when the match was in the balance, defined the entire season. When it mattered most, they fought to control the game and this finally resulted in three goals, first Smith, then Breust and finally Bradley Hill running on to the ball in the goal square to put us 30 points in front.

And talking of fighting Hawks, some observers questioned the recruitment of Brian Lake to Hawthorn, particularly after he and his wife were arrested in Sorrento over summer. Okay, it was just me, but I did add the caveat that – see page 10 – "it could be that both Brian and his better half are bringing to the club the sort of ruthless 'no-holds-barred' attitude that we need to succeed. In any case, I'll happily eat my words if my scepticism proves to be unfounded."

Consider those words eaten and digested.

The decision to recruit Brian Lake is being rightfully lauded. A Grand Final hero, he's the Stuart Dew of 2013, except that his slimming regime was more successful. But no less important was the decision the previous year to recruit the Gun, Jack Gunston. Lake certainly stopped goals at his end, but someone had to kick them at the other end and Gunston got on with doing just that in his own unassuming way, with his own very distinctive, very deliberate and deadly accurate kicking style. He's not the biggest, the strongest, the quickest or the most agile, yet he kicked 11 goals in the finals, compared to Roughead's four, Breust's three, Buddy's two and Rioli's one.

Trumpet solo ... bridge

Repeat

Our club song may not be the most stirring or memorable, or contain any elements of gritty urban groove or reach heights of anthemic grandeur (it's based on "Yankee Doodle", after all), or even include the word "girt", yet the team played to its message and truly lived up to its meaning on Grand Final Day. *Hawthorn ... the Musical*, anyone?

ICONIC MOMENTS

There's been a chorus of complaint from various commentators about the quality of the game. Apparently, it wasn't as spectacular as it could have been. These are the same journalists that, during the week, talked up Fremantle as likely premiers, completely overlooking that they play an über-defensive game based on no one scoring. It's a game plan that even Italian soccer would be embarrassed by. So I'm not sure what sort of spectacle these people were expecting.

Scott Gullan in the *Herald-Sun*, Martin Flanagan in *The Age* and the panel on *The Sunday Footy Show* were just a few who bemoaned that there were no "iconic" moments in the match. Let's ignore for the moment that "iconic", like "bespoke" (which, I hope you noticed, I used earlier), is one of the most overused and misused word in Australian media – it doesn't just mean "well-known", as some people seem to think. Hawthorn truly regrets this oversight. Take the cup away from us if you must. We must not have read the fine print and didn't realise that an entire season of hard work and effort also had to produce one particular incident that would look suitably dramatic when replayed ad nauseum in super-slo-mo for every footy promo during 2014.

But no "iconic" moments? I beg to differ. What about Isaac Smith's 60-metre goal in the final quarter? With the game in the balance and Hawthorn leading by 11 points, this goal set the MCG alight. I leapt from my seat as it went sailing through post-high. On the DVD version that comes with alternative commentaries, you get a sense that this was the kick that mattered. Commentating on Triple M, James Brayshaw said, "Oh, look out!" while SEN's Matt Granland shouted, "That is a monster! That's a huge kick for Hawthorn."

On Channel 7, Bruce McAvaney builds the drama as only he can: "Gee, it's a good kick. It is a great kick. It's one for the ages!"

But my favourite is Brian Taylor on 3AW, who bellows, "That is a thumping kick. That is a BIG BASTARD GOAL! Isaac Smith has nailed an absolute ripper from outside 50."

For me, "big bastard goal!" is the best description of a Grand Final moment since Michael Williamson shouted, "Jesaulenko – you beauty!" in 1970 as Jezza leapt over Graeme "Jerker" Jenkins to pull down the greatest mark of the twentieth century.

In other iconic moments, I'd nominate Luke Breust bursting from the pack moments after Smith's goal to kick another, Ben Stratton running down Ryan Crowley as he closed in on goal in the final quarter, Cyril's tackles, Gunston trapping the ball in the goal square late in the third and squeezing through his fourth to give us a decisive edge at three-quarter time, Brian Lake's series of intercepting marks. Need I go on?

I will then.

For Fremantle, Nathan Fyfe's three set shots that resulted in one behind and two out on the full. Nick Suban and Matthew Pavlich missing easy set shots, Luke McPharlin overstepping the mark by about two metres when Buddy was lining up in the first quarter.

And then there's Hayden Ballantyne's highlights package – dropping a chest mark 30 metres out from goal, slipping over in the middle of the ground, not giving off to Walters, who was by himself in the goal square, and then missing the shot, missing another set shot from 20 metres when the game was on the line, following up a few minutes later by missing one on the run ... All this from the man who was supposedly going to be the difference – well, he was, just not in the way people thought.

All of these are "iconic" moments worthy of replay on an endless loop in as little or as much super-slo-mo as you like. And what about the most iconic moment of all, when Hodgey and Clarko hoisted the cup heavenwards!

I feel a song coming on: "We're a happy team at Hawthorn ..."

Final scores: Hawthorn 11.11.77 d Fremantle 8.14.62

What we learned: The cultural cringe is still alive and well. While Hunters and Collectors provided the half-time entertainment, the Birds of Tokyo played pre-match. I didn't see them, I'm afraid; I was in the Tower 6 Bar, engaging in a bit of Grand Final ra ra, but really, why do we need to import these big bands from Japan to play on our special day? Oh, that's right, they're from Western Australia. Same difference.

I heard that Rihanna, who was in Australia at the time, expressed interest in performing at the Grand Final. How good would that have been? Sometimes getting the big international act isn't cultural cringe – it's just getting the big act. Rihanna would bring sass and near nudity to the occasion, and given that she's been receiving poor reviews for lip-synching, being drunk on stage and slurring her words, she sounds like a perfect fit for the Grand Final. She could have sung a duet with Meatloaf. Oh well, another missed opportunity.

What we already knew: You can take the boy out of Colac, but ... In his post-match speech, Luke Hodge tried to console the Freo boys, saying, "We know exactly how youse feel." *Youse*! You might excuse him for trying to use language he thought the players would understand, except that this is the second year in a row he's used "youse" as a collective pronoun in his post-Grand Final speech.

In Chapter 2 we examined how the number 23 would conspire to bring about premiership glory for Hawthorn. Numbers were crunched, algorithms run, cold facts forensically scrutinised and history consulted, and they all pointed to the same happy prophecy – that Hawthorn would be premiers.

Now that the season is over and the brown and gold confetti of 2013 has been brushed clear, another example of this truth is revealed. Hawthorn won 19 home-and-away games, three finals and one NAB cup match for the season – a total, you guessed it, of 23 victories.

11TH HEAVEN: HIGH ON HAWTHORN

Grand Final celebrations began immediately. Text messages began banking up on my phone. Short, sharp exultations of Hawks joy from friends and family. I returned a few to my sons, Oscar and Declan; to my wife, Angela; to my brothers; and Linda; and Julian; and possibly to one or two people I've never met. The ether was abuzz with electronic missives, the very air alive and humming with Hawthorn transmissions.

I headed to the Hugh Trumble Bar in the Members' for a celebratory Crown Lager with my brother Graeme and Geelong fan Murph. Then I caught up with Chan-Tha and Pete for the Hunters and Collectors concert and the presentation of the team. I somehow missed Birds of Tokyo again, but, truth be told, the only avian life I cared about this day were Hawks.

We danced, we sang, we waved our arms and rejoiced ... and the band hadn't even started yet. But when they did, they lit up the night opening with "Talking to a Stranger" – my favourite Hunnas song from their early art-rock period. Its opening line in French is from Baudelaire and means something about the men of the team amusing themselves. Probably best not to ask how, but quite apt nonetheless.

As for the rest of the weekend, we guzzled champagne like newborns take their milk, we relived the match, sang the song and headed to Glenferrie Oval on Sunday morning for the love-in. The presentation of the team and the cup was perhaps a little summary, but still satisfying. Gloating is good, and it's safe when you're among your own.

Having already resisted the urgings of the cashier at 7-Eleven to buy brown and gold-coated Krispy Kremes, I was also able to hold off joining the queues for premiership merchandise, which snaked around makeshift barriers. I didn't need to turn this into a commercial moment, to cheapen the experience by buying merchandise. Just knowing we were the premiers was enough, and I was happy to be suffused with this Buddhist-like sense of inner peace and oneness. Of course, when that wore off I'd throw my credit card at the Hawks Nest website and adorn my person and surroundings with every conceivable brown and gold memento of the big day.

Buddy lingering on stage with Cyril to deliver "whoops" and "yahoos" while pumping his arm in triumph was widely interpreted as a farewell to the fans. I tried my best to convince myself that his tears were not those of a man about to leave, but rather those of someone set to turn down a $10-million offer. I knew I was deluding myself, though.

Buddy had helped us win two premierships in his time at Hawthorn, so it was hard to begrudge him leaving. But nothing prepared me for the shock of what happened next.

SWAN DIVE – THE QUICK COMEDOWN

When Hawthorn won in 2008 the sense of euphoria lasted all summer. Perhaps it was that our victory on that day was unexpected, but even so, the day and its attendant feeling have stayed with me. I recall seeing Leonard Cohen, a long-time favourite, perform at Rochford Winery in the Yarra Valley in January of 2009, on a golden, sunny day not dissimilar to Grand Final Day 2008. Listening to Leonard sing his songs of profound understanding renewed for me the sense of enduring grace and transcendence I experienced when we won the flag in 2008.

In 2013, however, the news on the Tuesday after the match that Buddy Franklin was set to accept an offer of $10 million over nine years from the Sydney Swans brought about a very sudden and abrupt ending to any sense of premiership elation, replacing it instead with a despair and sense of hurt I hadn't expected.

This time the jubilation had lasted just two days. I haven't experienced a cocaine comedown or amphetamine freefall, but I can't imagine them to be any more deflating than the way I felt when I heard the news. Buddy going to GWS was one thing, but going to Sydney – the team that had beaten us in the previous year's Grand Final – felt like real betrayal. News that negotiations had begun a year ago made it feel even worse.

It is possible Clarkson coached him out of the club, forcing on him the role of team player and suppressing his virtuoso instincts. Throughout the year much was made by his team-mates and commentators, and even himself, that he was "playing a role". That's fine to a point, but we all know that, in society, "role play" is the domain of nerds and misfits, and boys in pilly jumpers who never get the girl. That doesn't sound like Buddy's style.

The consensus was that Buddy wanted to get out of Melbourne so he could live his life without his every move being reported in the media. Fair enough. Perhaps you have to have been subjected to that sort of media spotlight, with all its constraints and limitations, before you can appreciate what it is like. I mean, how often can you walk out your door to find a journo rifling through your bin before you get a bit sick of it? Or me flinging myself across the bonnet of your car whenever you tried to leave your driveway. I understand that this could become annoying. It began to hurt my ribs, too, after a while.

Others were blaming the influence of Buddy's Sydney-based girlfriend, model Jesinta Campbell, now referred to by Hawthorn fans on Twitter as Yoko.

It does seem, however, that Sydney simply doesn't have a salary cap. Or that they accept their living-away-from-home allowance, or living-outside-the-rules allowance, or whatever it's called, and then put all their players in a squat in Woolloomooloo. How else could they afford Tippett and Franklin on multi-million-dollar contracts in consecutive years?

And nine years seems like a deliberate strategy to simply scare off other bids or Hawthorn's willingness to match it. In the hours of frantic texting, tweeting and Facebooking when all of this was unfolding, I liked my friend Pete's suggestion the best: Hawthorn should match the offer and then trade him to GWS.

In truth, you can't blame Buddy for accepting $10 million over nine years. And you can't blame Sydney for wanting arguably the best forward in the competition.

I'll always wish the best for Buddy. He's given me as much joy and excitement as a Hawthorn fan as any other player I've seen – Matthews, Hudson, Brereton, Platten, Dunstall – and even in matches against Hawthorn, I hope he'll do well. I certainly won't boo him. But I retain sufficient bitterness that I don't care if the Sydney Swans send themselves broke and rot at the bottom of the ladder for a decade after Buddy retires.

The worst thing is I've now got to change all my passwords and PINs and get the giant "23" tattoo removed from my back. Unless Tim O'Brien, the new recruit who has been given the job of living up to the famous number, can add to its aura.

Perhaps it's time to fixate on another number. Number 11 shows potential. This is, after all, our 11th premiership, we were 11th on the ladder after Round 1, we defeated Geelong after 11 straight losses and we kicked 11.11 in the Grand Final. We also sacrificed two number 11s on the way: Clinton Young to Collingwood and Brendan Whitecross to injury.

OTHER DEPARTURES

Brent Guerra, Max Bailey and Michael Osborne have all retired, while Xavier Ellis has moved to the West Coast Eagles and Shane Savage to St Kilda.

That's three more from the great '08 team to leave (Guerra, Osborne and Ellis). Along with Buddy, that means there's only seven remaining. They're becoming as scarce as World War II veterans on Anzac Day. Savage, meanwhile, joins a long tradition of players who have represented both Hawthorn and St Kilda.

ETERNAL 2013 PREMIERS

Josh Gibson won the Peter Crimmins medal for Hawthorn's best and fairest, edging out Jarryd Roughead, second, and Sam Mitchell, third. All three played great seasons and any of them would have been a worthy winner. That means that in a team renowned for its attacking power, the two biggest individual awards were won by defenders: Josh Gibson the best and fairest, and Brian Lake the Norm Smith.

The distaste of the Buddy episode has already begun to fade. We'll grow accustomed to seeing him run around in the red back of the Swans jumper, we'll cheer when Gibbo fists it away from him or Lake outmarks him. We'll wear our "Premiers 2013" T-shirts until they are sweat-stained and threadbare, watch our Mark Knight *Herald-Sun* posters fade on bedroom windows over summer, plaster our cars with "Premiers 2013" stickers, and watch the video of the Grand Final again and again. And when we think of season 2013, we won't remember the

Buddy contract drama or the Essendon supplements saga; we won't recall the racism row or the Ashes loss, Miley Cyrus or the Melbourne coaching crisis; we'll forget about the federal election and the vagaries of the goal-review system. Those peripheral matters will fade from our memories, and as "we beat on, boats against the current, borne back ceaselessly into the past", as F. Scott Fitzgerald put it, what we'll remember is that Hawthorn are the premiers, and will remain eternal 2013 premiers.

PLAYERS WHO REPRESENTED HAWTHORN IN 2013

Alastair Clarkson – Coach

Jarryd Roughead – 2

Jordan Lewis – 3

Sam Mitchell – 5

Josh Gibson – 6

Michael Osborne – 7

Xavier Ellis – 8

Shaun Burgoyne – 9

Bradley Hill – 10

Brendan Whitecross – 11

Brad Sewell – 12

Kyle Cheney – 13

Grant Birchall – 14

Luke Hodge – 15 (captain)

Isaac Smith – 16

Brian Lake – 17

Brent Guerra – 18

Jack Gunston – 19

David Hale – 20

Shane Savage – 21

Luke Breust – 22

Lance Franklin – 23

Ben Stratton – 24

Ryan Schoenmakers -25

Liam Shiels – 26

Matt Spangher - 27

Paul Puopolo – 28

Will Langford – 29

Jonathan Simpkin – 32

Cyril Rioli – 33

Sam Grimley – 35

Jed Anderson – 37

Max Bailey – 39

Taylor Duryea – 41

Jonathon Ceglar - 47

ACKNOWLEDGEMENTS

I'd like to acknowledge the support of a number of people who helped make this book possible.

Firstly, my heartfelt thanks to Jacinta di Mase for her encouragement and guidance, and for making the book a reality.

Thank you also to the team at Nero and Black Inc. for their support and expertise in steering the project; in particular, Caitlin Yates, Jeanne Ryckmans, Elisabeth Young, Imogen Kandel, Chris Feik, Peter Long, Siân Scott-Clash, Duncan Blachford and Julian Welch.

I'm also greatly indebted to my editor, Jo Butler, for her keen insights and constructive suggestions.

Thanks to Trevor Marmalade and Tony Wilson, who each played a valuable role in bringing this project to life. And cheers to all the Hawthorn fans who submitted photos for inclusion in the book, and to Jon Spensley for the original idea for the photo section.

I'm grateful to my early readers, notably Linda Williamson and Julian Pocock, as well as Paul McKnight, who kick-started this book by urging me to write about Hawthorn.

A big high-five and premiership hug to my regular match-day companions Oscar Taylor, Chan-Tha Birch and Peter Delaney.

Thank you to my mother, Audrey, for giving me the freedom to follow my own path ... and my own team. I also acknowledge the key contribution and generosity of lifelong Hawthorn fan Jean Perkins, who nourished my childhood interest in Hawthorn by taking me to see them play.

Mostly, I offer my gratitude and devotion to my wife, Angela, and sons, Oscar and Declan, for their unwavering support and belief in me.

Finally, a big fist-pump to Alastair Clarkson and every player who donned the brown and gold for the mighty Hawks during the year. Go, Hawks!

Lightning Source UK Ltd.
Milton Keynes UK
UKOW06f1834190514

231920UK00011B/59/P